100 MOST DISGUSTING THINGS ON THE PLANET

Quarto is the authority on a wide range of topics.
Quarto educates, entertains and enriches the lives of
our readers—enthusiasts and lovers of hands-on living.
www.quartoknows.com

This library edition published in 2018 by Quarto Library,
an imprint of The Quarto Group.
6 Orchard Road, Suite 100
Lake Forest, CA 92630
T: +1 949 380 7510
F: +1 949 380 7575
www.QuartoKnows.com

Distributed in the United States and Canada by
Lerner Publisher Services
241 First Avenue North
Minneapolis, MN 55401 U.S.A.
www.lernerbooks.com

A CIP record for this book is available from the Library of Congress.

ISBN 978 1 68297 418 6

Manufactured in Dongguan, China TL092018
9 8 7 6 5 4 3 2 1

Cover: Corbis/Owen Franken; Shutterstock/Ivelin Radkov; © Dr. Nico J Smit/
University of Johannesburg, SA; Shutterstock/Paul
Prescott; Shutterstock/David Dohnal;
Corbis/Tim Davis; Ardea/Johan De
Meester; FLPA/Nigel Cattlin;
Photolibrary/James Robins

Anna Claybourne

100 MOST DISGUSTING THINGS ON THE PLANET

CONTENTS

INTRODUCTION

"Ewwwww! That's DISGUSTING!" You might hear someone saying that if they see you picking your nose or find stinky, rotten food in your fridge. But what exactly does it mean to be "disgusting"? The word *disgusting* literally means something that tastes bad or makes you feel sick. There are lots of things that can do this, as you'll see in this book. Foods you find revolting, icky body bits, nasty smells, and creepy-crawlies can all make you screw up your nose or back away in horror.

DISGUSTING TO YOU, DELIGHTFUL TO ME

A lot of "disgusting" things are only disgusting to some people and not to others. For example, someone who finds the idea of blue cheese completely revolting might be happy to munch on a fried grasshopper. Someone else might think eating grasshoppers is vile but love eating prawns, which would be extra-odd because grasshoppers and prawns actually belong to similar animal families—both have feelers, bulging eyes, and lots of wriggly legs.

WARNING!

This book describes a lot of unusual foods and other disgusting things. Whatever you do, do not try to copy anything you read in this book on your own. If you're in a restaurant that serves fried insects, for example, go ahead and try one. But don't try catching your own and eating it. It could be poisonous, dangerous, or carrying germs. It might even be an endangered species.

Snot, or mucus (see page 94), helps us to stay healthy, but we find it gross anyway.

LEARNING DISGUST

The truth is, we find many things disgusting because of our culture—the beliefs and values we grow up with. As a child, you learn what is disgusting from people around you yelling "Oh! That's gross," "Ewww," and "That's disgusting. Stop that at once!" In some cultures, for example, eating insects is normal; in others, people think it's so horrible that they couldn't do it if they tried.

DEFINITELY DISGUSTING

So, is disgustingness only in the eye of the beholder? Not always. For example, almost everyone in the world finds poo disgusting. It smells so bad that we instinctively know we need to keep away. This natural reaction protects us from the dangerous germs in poo and helps us to stay healthy.

TOILET HUMOR

When you were four or five, you probably thought it was incredibly funny to shout "poo!" Hey, maybe you still do! Maybe you're itching to turn to the rudest, yuckiest pages of this book and have a good giggle. This is normal, too. It's called toilet humor. In all cultures, there are things that are considered too private, rude, or disgusting to talk about. Because they are forbidden, people—especially children—often find them fascinating and funny. Go ahead, turn the page!

Many wild animals have their own revolting habits. Hippopotamuses, for example (see page 37), spin their tails around when they poo, spraying muck everywhere!

YUCK FACTOR

😝	A little gross
😝 😝	Eww!
😝 😝 😝	Yuck!
😝 😝 😝 😝	Really revolting
😝 😝 😝 😝 😝	Totally disgusting!

DISGUSTING

From dung-munching beetles to flesh-eating maggots, from vomit-squirting baby birds to jelly-squirting cucumbers, from stinky mushrooms to plants that can gobble up a mouse—the natural world is full of

NATURE

truly gross living things. Of course, many of them are disgusting only to us—as far as they are concerned, they just survive, like all life on Earth. Read on to find out more about their horrible habits.

COCKROACH

You open your cupboard and reach in for a packet of pasta—uururrrgggggh! It's CRAWLING with cockroaches! Cockroaches (or "roaches") are insects that look similar to beetles. Like mice, they love sharing our homes and our food. They often make people jump, shudder, or run screaming from the room! But how revolting are they, really?

DISEASE SPREADERS

Cockroaches do some really disgusting things. They can spread dangerous disease germs. And if there's a big cockroach infestation, they can also give off a vile smell, which comes from cockroach poo and dead cockroach bodies. Yuck!

SPEEDY-CRAWLIES

Cockroaches can run really fast—and this may be one reason why people find them so unnerving. A cockroach can skitter across your floor at 3.5 miles per hour (5.6 km/h). Considering how small a cockroach is, that's like a human running at over 190 miles per hour (300 km/h). And even weirder, to reach their top speed, some roaches stand up like humans and run on their hind legs.

Cockroaches feast on someone's half-eaten sandwich.

YUCK FACTOR!

No one loves them, but cockroaches only bother you if you give them food.

TOP TIP! To keep cockroaches away, keep all your food wrapped and sealed well. Always wipe up spilled food, so there's nothing for them to nibble.

DID YOU KNOW?

A cockroach can survive for several weeks without eating—and even without its head!

BLOWFLY

As flies go, adult blowflies are not disgusting to look at—they're amazingly beautiful, with their bright, metallic bodies in jewel-like blue and green. But what we do find disgusting is baby blowflies—otherwise known as **MAGGOTS!**

DEAD MEAT

Female blowflies seek out dead animals by their stinky smell and then lay their eggs in them. The eggs hatch into small, white, wriggly maggots, which look a bit like grains of rice. They feed on the rotting flesh and grow bigger and bigger. A dead sheep or rat can often be seething with maggots.

ON THE MOVE

Next, the maggots have to pupate, or go into a cocoon, to turn into adults. They leave the rotting body and wriggle off in search of a good dry, safe place to pupate. If there's a dead mouse hidden somewhere in your house, the first sign might be when you find the maggots marching across the floor!

YUCK FACTOR!

Writhing, wriggling maggots are totally harmless, but can make some people feel ill!

CRIME CRACKERS

Forensic scientists can use maggots to find out how long ago someone was murdered. They can tell by how big the maggots in the body have grown.

Maggots cluster together in tight gaps and wriggle in disgusting, shiny heaps.

HOUSEFLY

Mmm, you've just come indoors after playing outside and there's a tasty-looking cupcake sitting on the kitchen table. Should you eat it? Why not?! Well, if it's been sitting there uncovered in warm weather, a really disgusting housefly could have buzzed by and had a taste first. And here's what THAT involves. . . .

FLY FEAST

Houseflies have spongelike mouths that can only soak up liquid food. So, after landing on your cake, a housefly spits and vomits onto it, to make the food mushy and break it down into liquid. When it's nice and runny, the fly sucks up as much as it can, leaving some spit

MUCKY MAGGOTS

Like blowflies, houseflies lay eggs that hatch into wriggly maggots. They lay their eggs in rubbish or animal poo, which the maggots feed on.

and vomit behind. While feeding, flies also poo constantly, so they leave that behind, too!

DISEASES

As they buzz around, flies can pick up all kinds of germs and parasites, such as deadly food-poisoning bacteria on raw meat, or botfly eggs (see page 13). They then leave these everywhere they land, so they can spread lots of nasty diseases.

TOP TIP! Keep all your food wrapped, covered, or in the fridge, especially in warm weather, unless you want it covered in fly spit, poo, and disgusting germs!

Buzzing, slurping houseflies feast on ham that has been left uncovered.

YUCK FACTOR!

Few creatures spoil your lunch quite as badly as a housefly.

BOTFLY

If you think blowfly and housefly maggots are disgusting, it's about to get a whole lot worse. Botfly maggots don't live in old, rotting meat. They don't live in garbage, and they don't live in poo. They live inside, and feed on, other living animals—including horses, cows . . . and humans. Totally gross!

EGGS ON YOUR SKIN

Botflies want to get their eggs onto the skin of their host (the animal they invade). They sometimes lay them directly on another animal's skin. But human botflies lay their eggs on an insect such as a housefly or mosquito, which then leaves them on human skin.

BURROWING IN

When a botfly egg hatches, the maggot immediately burrows under the skin and hangs on with tiny hooklike parts. It feeds on blood, growing fatter and fatter. At last, it lets go and drops out of its host's skin onto the ground, ready to turn into an adult fly.

...is is what a botfly maggot looks like once it's ...en pulled out of its cozy nest in your skin!

WHAT'S IT LIKE? Most people don't notice a botfly maggot in their skin at first—they just think it's an insect bite. But as the maggot grows, it feels horribly itchy, painful, and sometimes wriggly! You can also see a tiny airhole on the skin that the maggot uses to breathe.

TARANTULA

Many people fear and loathe spiders and find them revolting. Scientists are not sure why, but if you do feel like this about spiders, the most horrible of all are probably tarantulas—the biggest, fattest, and hairiest spiders in the world.

ARE THEY MONSTERS?

Tarantulas look terrifying, but they aren't actually the most dangerous spiders. Most can give you an unpleasant bite, about as bad as a bee sting—but they are not killers. They can be quite disgusting, though. They have sharp fangs that inject poison into their prey, and like some other creatures, they dribble digestive chemicals onto their food to liquefy it before sucking up the juice. They roll the dried-up leftovers into a tidy little ball. What nice manners!

HORRIBLY HAIRY

A tarantula's hairs help it sense other animals nearby by detecting vibrations from their movements. Many tarantulas also have special stinging hairs to repel predators. Some can actually flick these hairs right off their bodies at any animal

A tarantula devours a grasshopper.

YUCK FACTOR!

They look hairy and scary, but only some people find them revolting—others keep them as pets!

that attacks them. These hairs can kill some small animals. They also give humans a nasty skin rash, and are dangerous if you breathe them in or get them in your eyes.

DID YOU KNOW?

The world's biggest spider, the Goliath bird-eating spider, is a tarantula with a leg span of up to 12 inches (30 cm). It can kill and eat small birds, lizards, frogs, and mice!

TARANTULA HAWK WASP

Worse than any tarantula is the tarantula hawk wasp. The female hunts tarantulas, paralyzing them with a potent sting. But she doesn't eat them. She drags the still-living spider into a burrow and lays her egg on it so that her baby has a fresh food supply.

EATEN ALIVE

When the larva, or baby wasp, hatches from the egg, it starts sucking bodily fluids from the tarantula's paralyzed body. Then, as it grows bigger and stronger, it burrows into the tarantula's body, eating it alive. It saves the organs for last, to keep the spider alive and fresh for as long as possible!

DIFFERENT DINNER

Adult tarantula hawk wasps don't eat meat. They feed on nectar and rotting fruits that contain alcohol, making them dizzy and unable to fly!

Here, a tarantula hawk wasp approaches its much larger prey, a big, hairy tarantula.

SIZE AND STRENGTH

Tarantula hawks are big for wasps—about 2 inches (5 cm) long—but not as big as most tarantulas. They can sting and drag tarantulas much bigger than themselves.

YUCK FACTOR!

Eating a whole spider that's still alive is a gross way to grow up!

TOP TIP! If you see one of these giant wasps, keep away. They have huge stingers, and if they zap you it's incredibly painful.

This is not a terrifying space robot, but the face of a tarantula hawk wasp.

VELVET WORM

Velvet worms are weird creatures found in caves and undergrowth in damp, tropical parts of the world. They're not large, but they have icky hunting and feeding habits that allow them to prey on spiders, snails, insects, and other worms much bigger than themselves.

CREEPY AND CRAWLY

Velvet worms are similar to earthworms—they're long, wriggly, and squishy—but unlike earthworms, they have up to 86 short, chubby legs. They got their name because their skin is covered in fine bristles and scales that feel velvety to the touch. They range from the size of a grain of rice to 6 inches long, but however big they are, all velvet worms are fierce hunters.

TIME FOR LUNCH!

Velvet worms like darkness and usually hunt by night. They slither around sniffing out things to eat, using their highly sensitive antennae. Once a velvet worm smells its prey, it sneaks silently toward it. The prey may know nothing until the worm is right next to it.

SPLURT!

Suddenly, the worm shoots lots of white, sticky, gluey stuff all over its victim from two swiveling squirters on the sides of its head. As soon as the glue is exposed to the air, it starts to harden, trapping the prey and holding it still. The velvet worm slices up its meal with supersharp jaws and gobbles up the bits. Munch!

YUCK FACTOR!

This is one worm you don't want to meet on a dark night.

Squirt! This sticky glue will trap the velvet worm's prey.

AARRGGH! MY EYES! Velvet worms cannot bear bright light. If you shine a flashlight at one, it will scuttle away into a dark crevice.

POO-COVERED BEETLE

Several species of beetle have a strange habit that would certainly be disgusting if we ever tried it! They give their babies a lovely, thick coating of poo, to protect them from deadly predators.

SMELLY EGGS

The baby beetles get their first stinky covering before they even hatch. After laying her eggs, the mother beetle carefully spreads her own poo all over them. It then hardens into a solid protective shell—lucky babies!

DOES IT WORK?

Scientists have tried testing these larvae to see if their poo blanket really does put off predators. It does! Both young chickens and hunting ants refused to eat the poo-coated beetle babies.

POO ARMOR

Once each larva, or baby beetle, hatches, it keeps the shell-like covering from its egg and adds to it using its own poo. Depending on the species, the larva covers itself with poo in the form of blobs, strings, or sticky goop. It forms a kind of armor plating, which scientists call a "fecal shield."

This tiny but stinky pile of poo is actually a tortoise beetle larva, hiding beneath its protective poo shield.

YUCK FACTOR!

It sounds disgusting, but the hardened poo shell isn't all that bad—not as stinky as dog poo!

MILLIPEDE

Millipedes are the ultimate creepy-crawlies. They have more legs than any other animal on Earth. Their legs ripple in a wavelike pattern as they glide and slither smoothly through leaf litter and soil. They are mostly harmless, but many people are horrified by their shiny, plump bodies and tiny, wriggly legs—especially if they meet a giant millipede!

YUCK FACTOR!

Like many creepy-crawlies, millipedes can look scary and horrible, but they're not that bad!

MUD MUNCHER

Like earthworms, millipedes mostly mind their own business, burrowing through soil and rotting plants, munching as they go. They don't hunt or eat other animals, and if they're in danger they curl up into a tight coil.

LEAKING ACID

However, if under attack, some millipede species can release a stinging, burning liquid, or even a poisonous gas, from tiny openings along their bodies. It's strong enough to burn human skin, and it's good for putting off hungry millipede hunters like birds.

MONSTER MILLIPEDES

Most millipedes are only a few centimeters long. But the giant African millipede is a monster that can grow to be over 12 inches (30 cm) long and is as thick as your thumb.

DID YOU KNOW?

Most millipedes only have between 50 and 400 legs, but one was found to have 750!

Imagine how this enormous millipede must tickle as all its tiny legs skitter over your hands!

ASSASSIN BUG

The assassin bug certainly lives up to its name. This disgusting creepy-crawly likes nothing more than devouring its fellow insects alive by injecting them with spit that dissolves their insides, then slurping them up like a fresh smoothie.

YUCK FACTOR!

This beastly bug has a seriously revolting way of getting its lunch.

Brightly colored assassin bugs crawl over a leaf in a rain forest in Central America.

STABBING STRAW

The assassin bug's mouth is shaped like a long, sharp, flexible straw. It's so strong that it can puncture the hard exoskeleton, or shell-like covering, of other insects such as beetles. It sneaks up and stabs them in the back when they aren't looking, sometimes grabbing hold of them with its sticky feet, too.

LIQUEFIED!

Next, the bug squirts its digestive juices into its prey's body, turning its insides to liquid. Then all the bug has to do is suck it all up, leaving an empty husk. Their hunting technique lets assassin bugs feed on insects much bigger than themselves.

KISS FROM A BUG

At least assassin bugs are too small to eat humans! Well, not quite. Some assassin bugs, found in North and Central America, will also attack humans while they sleep, stabbing a soft body part, such as the lip, and sucking out some blood. Because of this they are called "kissing bugs." Lovely!

Aaarrgggh! There's no hope for this ladybug as an assassin bug spears it and sucks out its insides.

TOP TIP! As well as being disgusting, kissing bugs can spread a serious disease called Chagas' disease. So don't forget your mosquito net!

BOMBARDIER BEETLE

Don't mess with a bombardier beetle! If it thinks it's in danger, this little beetle will quickly swivel its rear end toward you and shoot out a deadly spray—an explosive mixture of hot, revolting-smelling liquid and gas that can badly burn your skin.

HOW DOES IT DO IT?

The beetle's body contains two tiny tanks, each filled with a different chemical. When danger threatens, the beetle squeezes these two chemicals into another chamber, where they combine and cause a chemical reaction that makes heat and gas. The pressure from the gas makes the mixture shoot out of the beetle's behind.

YUCK FACTOR!

A jet of boiling-hot beetle spray is more funny than disgusting!

WHO FEARS THE SPRAY?

Bombardier beetles aren't really very dangerous to humans, though an attack can hurt and make your skin blister. But their ferocious spurt of chemicals can seriously injure or even kill small hunting animals, like spiders or frogs, that prey on beetles.

DID YOU KNOW?

The bombardier doesn't just shoot once, but 500 or more times in quick succession, all within a split second. When it attacks, you can hear a popping or hissing sound.

A bombardier can swivel its tail end around to aim its weapon anywhere.

DUNG BEETLE

A dung beetle spends its life seeking out one thing—smelly, sticky dung (animal poo). To a dung beetle, dung is a source of food and a place to lay its eggs so that its babies can feed on bits of chewed, pooed-out plants in the dung as they grow.

SOIL HELPERS

Dung beetles actually do a very useful job for us. The dirty poo they tidy away and bury in the ground makes the soil more fertile for growing crops.

"I SMELL DUNG!"

Dung beetles find their dung, usually from plant-eating animals such as cows, using their sense of smell. Or they follow animals around and sit patiently, waiting for them to make a poo.

DUNG BALLS

Some dung beetles live in piles of dung, but most shape it into neat balls, roll it away, and bury it in the ground to keep it safe. Then they lay eggs inside the dung ball and guard the babies as they grow inside it.

FASCINATING FACTS

- Dung beetles often try to steal each other's precious dung balls and have fights over them.
- When a beetle rolls a dung ball away, it moves in a totally straight line to get away from other beetles using as little energy as possible. At night, it uses the moon for navigation—its own kind of GPS!
- To the ancient Egyptians, dung beetles were sacred—they represented the sun god, Ra, rolling the sun across the sky each day.

YUCK FACTOR!

Dung is yucky to us, but by eating and burying it, dung beetles help get rid of it!

Mmm, dinner! Dung beetles zero in on a fresh pile of dung.

GIANT ISOPOD

**It has a face like an alien, with giant, glittery, reflective eyes.
It has 14 jointed, creepy-crawly legs. It looks very like a pale, purplish gray wood louse—and in fact it is closely related to wood lice—but it grows to almost 16 inches (40 cm) long, the size of a domestic cat. You might be pleased to hear that this monstrous creature lives in the sea, so you won't be finding it under a stone in your yard—but many people still find the giant isopod one of the ugliest and most revolting creatures on the planet.**

DEEP DOWN

The giant isopod lives on the deep seabed, where it creeps through the muddy ooze, scavenging dead sea creatures. Like many scavengers, it can go a long time without food, then fill itself to the brim when it gets the chance. When they lay eggs, female isopods grow a special pouch, like a kangaroo's, to hold the eggs and newly hatched babies.

IN CAPTIVITY

Giant isopods sometimes get caught in deepwater trawling nets or special traps. Some people keep them in tanks at home as pets, and there are some aquariums where you can see living specimens on public display.

This giant isopod lives in the deep, icy-cold waters around the Antarctic.

DID YOU KNOW?

In some parts of Asia, giant isopods are considered a delicacy. Like wood lice, they are related to crabs and lobsters, and their meat tastes similar to lobster.

SLUGS AND SNAILS

Eeeerrrrggghh! The feeling of a cold, damp, slimy slug on your skin is repellent. Slugs and snails feel this way because of the sticky, slippery slime that oozes out of them wherever they go. We also find their soft, squishy bodies horrible when we accidentally step on and squash one.

WHY SO SLIMY?

Slugs and snails secrete most of their slime from the underside of their tough, crawling "foot." It lets them slide along smoothly and helps them climb up walls and plants on which they feed. They also have slime all over their bodies, which is good for slipping out of the grip of hungry birds.

HMM, WHO'S BEEN HERE?

Snails and slugs can sniff each other's slime to find out which species they each come from. This helps them find a mate of the same species as themselves.

SNAIL SNACKS

Snails are a well-known favorite food in France, where they are baked with garlic butter. They are also a popular food in parts of Africa, where the giant African land snail can grow up to 8 inches (20 cm) long.

STOMACH FEET

Slugs and snails may look different, but they are actually very similar. A snail is just a slug with a shell. Both belong to an animal family called the gastropods, meaning "stomach feet."

You can see the slimy undersides of these two snails as they coil around a plant stem.

Both snails and slugs have eyes on the ends of two feelers, or "tentacles."

GIANT JELLYFISH

How big can a jellyfish get?
The biggest of all, the Nomura's jellyfish of Japan and the lion's mane jellyfish found in northern oceans, can grow 6–7 feet (2 m) across. That's wider than a man is tall! The lion's mane jellyfish can also be very long, with tentacles sometimes growing to an incredible 120 feet (36 m).

FRILLY, SLIMY, AND STRINGY

Many people find jellyfish strange and disgusting to look at. They have jellylike, dome-shaped bodies. Tentacles and flappy armlike parts dangle down from the underside, surrounding the jellyfish's mouth, which is in the middle.

Many jellyfish can give you a dangerous sting with their tentacles, but giant jellyfish are not usually as deadly as some smaller jellyfish. They don't feed on humans, and people don't usually get caught in them.

JELLYFISH PLAGUES

In the past few years, huge swarms of giant Nomura's jellyfish have been causing problems for Japanese fishing boats. They get caught in fishing nets, covering the fish with slime and jellyfish poison so that they can't be eaten.

A diver attaches a sensor to a Nomura's jellyfish in Japan.

STARFISH

What happens when a starfish wants to eat a tasty fish or sea slug, but it's too big? Simple! The starfish simply turns its stomach inside out, making it poke right out of its body through its mouth, and wraps it around its prey. The stomach then releases strong digestive juices that dissolve the unlucky victim alive. The starfish's stomach sucks up the dissolved prey and passes it to a second, smaller stomach inside its body.

STOMACH INVASION

Even having a strong shell doesn't protect other sea creatures from a marauding starfish stomach. Some types of starfish can use powerful suckers on their arms to pry open shellfish like clams and mussels. Then they insert their stomachs right into the gap and start digesting and liquefying the creature hiding inside!

SHOULD I BE SCARED?

The starfish's hunting method is bad news for a lot of sea creatures, and it's certainly disgusting. But the good news for us is that they don't gobble up humans. Most starfish are small—they range from about 1 inch (2 cm) to about 20 inches (50 cm) across—and they can only wrap their stretchy stomachs around things that move slowly. So you won't have your hand liquefied while going for a swim!

NEW ARMS

Starfish really can regenerate, or grow, a new arm if one is chopped off. It's even true that if a single starfish is cut into two pieces, each piece can regenerate, making two new starfish.

This starfish is using its curling arms to ensnare its prey—Antarctic krill.

YUCK FACTOR!

An inside-out stomach on the prowl is a horrible thought!

KOMODO DRAGON

The Komodo dragon isn't a real dragon. It's far more disgusting than that! This is the world's biggest lizard, growing up to 10 feet (3 m) long. It looks a bit like a short-legged, small-headed dinosaur, with a long, heavy tail and a forked tongue.

IN SEARCH OF DEAD MEAT

Komodo dragons are mainly scavengers and eat dead flesh, but they do hunt and kill as well. Like snakes, they stick out their tongues to detect scents in the air and can sniff out a rotting carcass from over 5 miles (8 km) away. When they find their prey, such as a dead or dying goat or pig, they guzzle it in big chunks or even swallow it whole.

YUCK FACTOR!

This creature's table manners are among the world's worst, and it has terribly stinky breath, too.

DID YOU KNOW?

Komodo dragons have been known to dig up human graves to eat the bodies inside. Local people pile stones on top of graves to stop this from happening.

GERMS AND POISON

Komodos can also kill living creatures—either by infecting them with disgusting disease germs from their mouths or by injecting them with venom.

PUTRID PELLETS

After eating an animal, the Komodo dragon vomits up a "gastric pellet"—a lump of indigestible bits of fur, teeth, and bones. Urgh!

Komodo dragons like this one live only on a few islands in Indonesia, where tourists often go to view them.

HORNED LIZARD

This bizarre desert lizard, found in North America, has a really revolting trick for scaring off predators that want to eat it. It squirts them with a well-aimed jet of blood from its eyes!

HORNED AND DANGEROUS

These lizards are small, reaching only around 2.5–6.5 inches (6.4–16.5 cm) in length—but their horns, frills, spines, and spotted, speckled skin make them look like miniature dragons or dinosaurs. Their spikes alone can put off some predators—they can puff up their bodies to make themselves bigger and spikier. They also have a secret weapon. . . .

BLOOD SQUIRTER

The horned lizard can shoot its own blood a distance of up to 3 feet (1 m) away to frighten an attacker. How? The blood flow from its head to its body is cut off, so that the blood collects and pressure builds up. When the pressure is strong enough, weak blood vessels right next to the lizard's eyes burst open, and the blood spurts out.

UGH! WHAT WAS THAT?

The jet of blood might confuse a predator, like a wildcat or coyote, when it lands in its eyes or face. The blood also tastes revolting to some animals.

AN AMAZING DISCOVERY

Spanish explorer Francisco Hernandez first described the horned lizard in 1651: "If its head or eyes are pressed," he wrote, "or if it is struck carelessly, it vigorously shoots drops of blood . . . up to a distance of three paces."

Splat! Blood squirts from a horned lizard's eye.

YUCK FACTOR!

It's a blood-squirting, horny-headed monster!—but only in miniature.

CANE TOAD

With their bulging eyes and bumpy, poisonous skin, all toads are quite disgusting. But the cane toad is probably the yuckiest of all. Huge, ugly, and deadly poisonous, cane toads have become a nightmare in several places. In Australia, they were introduced to help farmers by eating beetles that fed on farm crops. But unfortunately, they also poison wildlife, pets, and farm animals.

WARTY!

An old wives' tale says that because toads are covered in warts, you can catch warts yourself by touching a toad. But it's nonsense! The bumps on toads' backs aren't real warts at all. They are glands, a kind of small body organ. They release poisons that help protect toads from predators.

KILLER TOADS

Cane toads have two extra-large glands, one behind each eye. If the toad is attacked, these glands release a poisonous, milky white substance. In some animals, including humans, the poison causes drooling and stops the heart from working. It can be fatal. Cane toads' eggs and tadpoles are deadly poisonous, too.

DID YOU KNOW?

Some dogs and other animals like licking cane toads, because the poison makes them feel pleasantly dizzy! This is dangerous and unhealthy.

A cane toad can grow to almost 12 inches (30 cm) long. This one is enjoying a frog as a snack.

TOP TIP! If your dog or cat bites a cane toad, rinse the pet's mouth out with water and take it to a vet as soon as you can.

SURINAM TOAD

The Surinam toad, despite its name, is actually a frog found in rivers and ponds in South America. It has one of the most amazing ways of giving birth—it's so strange, it seems like something from a sci-fi movie.

LEAF FROG The Surinam toad has a strange body shape, too—almost completely flat, like a leaf.

LAYING EGGS

The female toad lays around 100 eggs. As she lays them, the male toad collects them and presses them onto her back, where they stick to her skin. Over the next few hours, the eggs sink into the female's back, and skin grows right over them.

BABIES

In the little pockets under the female's skin, the eggs hatch and grow. The mother's back swells as this happens, and the pockets get bigger and push together, making a honeycomb pattern. After several months, the baby frogs shoot out of their chambers and swim free. By now each baby is around 1 inch (2 cm) long. They can usually burst out by themselves, but if they aren't strong enough, the mother can use her back muscles to push them out. Pop!

YUCK FACTOR!

When the froglets burst out from under their mother's skin, they look disgusting and scary!

A mother Surinam toad with her back covered in pockets, containing baby frogs growing under her skin.

HAGFISH

This extremely weird, snake-shaped fish is probably the slimiest thing in the world. If it is touched or threatened, its skin releases a sticky substance that combines with seawater to make masses of slippery slime. It completely covers the hagfish, making it very hard for predators to hold on.

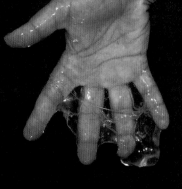

This brave person dipped their hand in hagfish slime to show just how slimy, sticky, and disgusting it is!

FLESH EATERS

Hagfish are scavengers. When a sea creature such as a whale dies and sinks to the ocean floor, they start burrowing into it, munching as they go. But they sometimes do this to living sea creatures, too! Large fish often swim around with a few hagfish burrowing into and nibbling away at their bodies. Ugh!

A hagfish's face has sharp teeth for biting into flesh, surrounded by sensitive parts called barbels, which the hagfish uses to feel its way around.

TIED UP IN KNOTS

Another strange thing the hagfish can do is tie itself into a knot. It can slide the knot up and down its body. It does this to pull itself out of a dead animal or out of a predator's grip. It can use the same trick to clear old slime off itself, too.

YUCK FACTOR!

Scientists and fishermen often call the hagfish the most disgusting creature in the sea. It's truly revolting!

Blobfishes are occasionally dragged up from the deep oceans by trawling nets.

BLOBFISH

This crazy-looking deep-sea fish doesn't actually do anything disgusting. It just looks amazingly odd and ugly, like a blobby, big-nosed cartoon!

JELLY BELLY

This freaky fish really does deserve the name "blob." Most of its body is made up of a strange, wobbly, jellylike substance, and it has hardly any muscles.

DEEP-SEA DWELLER

The blobfish lives in water as much as 2,625 feet (800 m) deep—which explains why it is rarely seen, and why people know so little about it. At these depths, there is a huge amount of water pressure pushing on the fish from all sides. Other fish float using a pocket of gas in their bodies called a swim bladder, or stop themselves from sinking by making sure they keep moving all the time. But the blobfish works in a different way. Its blobby jelly body allows it to drift slowly along just above the seabed, suspended in the water. It doesn't move fast or go hunting for food—it just eats scraps of food that float by.

CHICKEN FISH

Like a chicken, the blobfish lays its eggs in a nest on the seabed and sits on them until they hatch.

YUCK FACTOR!

It's a bit cruel to call this fatheaded fish really revolting. It's just funny-looking!

VULTURE

In cartoons, vultures circle in the sky above people who are lost in the desert, waiting for them to die so that they can swoop down and start eating them. Is it true?

Vultures do circle, but mainly just to look for food. They are scavengers that feed on carrion—old, rotting dead bodies. They can spot these from high in the sky and can also smell rotting flesh.

I'M STUFFED!

Vultures often live in desert areas, and they can go for days or even weeks without food. So, when they do find a tasty rotting carcass, they eat as much as they possibly can. They stuff themselves so full, they can't fly or even move! They have to sit on the ground until their dinner is digested.

WHY AREN'T THEY ILL?

Rotting meat contains revolting bacteria that can make humans, and many other animals, very ill. Vultures don't care, though—their superstrong stomachs are not affected by the germs. However, they do sometimes die when they eat farm animals that have been given medicines, which are poisonous to them.

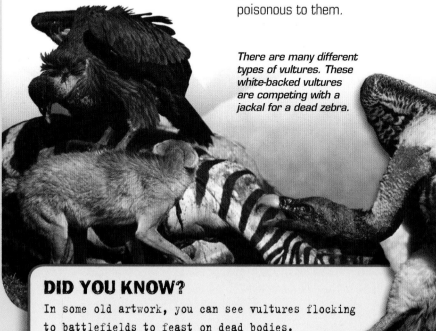

There are many different types of vultures. These white-backed vultures are competing with a jackal for a dead zebra.

DID YOU KNOW?

In some old artwork, you can see vultures flocking to battlefields to feast on dead bodies.

FULMAR

YUCK FACTOR!

😖 😖 😖 😖

The fulmar chick's squirty, stinky slime makes it one of the most disgusting birds on the planet.

You're a fearless wildlife explorer, scaling a windblown coastal crag to photograph wild seabirds in their cliff-top nests. You reach the top and find yourself face-to-face with a white, fluffy fulmar chick. Cuuuute!

But suddenly—SPLAT! The chick squirts slimy, oily, orangey yellow, fishy-smelling vomit out of its stomach right into your eyes and mouth. Bleeuurrrgggh!

DISGUSTING DEFENSE

Fulmars lay just one egg at a time, and the newly hatched chick is left alone in its nest while its parents go fishing for food. The chicks use their vile vomit-squirting skills to defend themselves from attackers while their parents are away.

DEADLY FEATHER-FOULER

The vomit is actually mostly made up of a kind of thick, gloppy oil that collects in seabirds' stomachs after they eat fish. As well as smelling foul, the oil can clog other birds' feathers, making them so matted that they can't fly. This can be dangerous, even deadly, for a hunting bird such as a skua or eagle.

SHARPSHOOTER

Baby fulmars can shoot their vomit very accurately into an intruder's eyes. They can also fire it a distance of 6–10 feet (2–3 m).

Caught on camera, a fulmar chick's stream of vomit flies out of its throat through the air.

TOP TIP! Wildlife experts and climbers who do get up close to fulmars have to keep their distance to avoid a fish-oil shower. Wearing sunglasses can protect your eyes.

FIELDFARE

It's an innocent-looking, brown-speckled songbird that you might see in your yard. But if you get too close to its eggs, the fieldfare can turn nasty. It keeps away predators who want to steal its eggs by deliberately shooting a stream of slimy bird poo all over them. Yuck!

PROTECTION FOR EVERYONE

Smaller birds have caught on to the fieldfare's cunning tactics and often build their own nests near the fieldfare's. This helps their eggs stay safe from egg-stealing predators, too.

GET OFF MY EGGS!

Birds' eggs can provide a feast for predators such as bigger birds, snakes, and squirrels. They hang around birds' nests hoping to help themselves to a snack. When the fieldfare sees this happening, it flies up high, then dive-bombs its enemy. At the last second, it swoops upward, so that it can aim its rear end at the predator, then fires its poo.

BIRD BOMBER

The fieldfare's poo-shooting defense works best on other birds, such as crows. Like the fulmar chick's vomit (see page 33), sticky fieldfare poo may clog up birds' feathers and stop them from flying. It's less effective on four-legged hunters such as stoats.

YUCK FACTOR!

Bird poo is horribly sticky and slimy and can contain disgusting germs. Keep away!

This fieldfare mother will protect her nest and eggs fiercely.

VAMPIRE BAT

Scary bats that fly by night and creep into your bed to suck your blood exist only in horror stories—right? WRONG! Vampire bats are real, and they do feed on fresh blood. Their disgusting diet comes mainly from animals such as cows and goats. But one species, the common vampire bat, is also happy to suck human blood.

TOP TIP! If you are in Central or South America, beware the risk of vampire bats. To protect yourself, keep doors and windows closed at night, or sleep under a mosquito net.

A vampire bat licks up a flow of blood from its victim—in this case a chicken.

CREEPING AND CRAWLING

To avoid waking you up and having its meal ruined, a vampire bat will land some distance away, then creep silently toward you, using its folded-up wings as feet. Yikes!

RAZOR-SHARP TEETH!

Once it's close to you, the bat uses its sharp fangs to cut open your skin. It has special saliva (spit) that numbs pain, so you don't feel a thing. Then, as your blood flows out, the bat quickly laps it up. *Slurp!*

REVOLTING RABIES

Being bitten by a vampire bat won't harm you much—unless the bat is carrying rabies. This is a disgusting (and deadly) disease that makes you foam at the mouth (produce lots of spit bubbles).

Check out these fangs!

DID YOU KNOW?

Feeding fills a vampire bat with so much blood that it's too heavy to fly. So it waits a while, digests its dinner, then makes itself lighter by having a big pee before taking flight.

YUCK FACTOR!

😖 😖 😖 😖

Bloodsucking bats are pretty revolting—and scary, too.

SKUNK

Anyone who's unlucky enough to have been sprayed by a skunk can tell you that it's one of the most disgusting smells in the entire animal kingdom.

A skunk makes a special stinky, oily liquid in its anal glands—two small organs on its rear end. As a defense, it will cover anything that threatens it in this revolting gunk. And it certainly works. Skunk spray can even put off hunting animals that are much larger than the skunk itself.

WHAT'S IT SMELL LIKE?

The smell of skunk spray resembles a mixture of rotting eggs, burning plastic, garlic, and sewage (that's old, rotting waste from toilets—see page 105)! As well as smelling really bad, it can make your eyes water and make you choke or vomit. Let's hope you never have to smell it for yourself!

STINK SHOOTER

A skunk can even get you from a distance. Strong muscles around the glands squeeze together to shoot the liquid up to 16 feet (5 m) away. Cunningly, the skunk usually avoids getting any of the smelly goop on its own fur.

A skunk may stamp its feet or stick its tail in the air to warn you that it's about to spray.

DID YOU KNOW?

If clothes or other objects are sprayed by a skunk, it's pretty much impossible to wash the smell out.

HIPPOPOTAMUS

Maybe you think of a hippo as an innocent, lumbering beast. Not pretty, but not all that disgusting, either. Well, you're wrong. Hippos have so many disgusting habits, it's hard to know where to begin!

HIPPO HALITOSIS

First of all, hippos are famous for their terrible breath. Like cows, they munch huge amounts of grass, which ferments in their stomachs and gives off smelly gases. Many male hippos also have damaged and rotting teeth from fighting one another. The result—bad breath and disgustingly stinky burps!

SWEATING BLOOD!

When outsiders first saw hippos in Africa, they thought they sweated blood because their skin leaks droplets of red, sticky fluid. This isn't actually blood, but a chemical that kills germs on the hippo's skin and also protects it from the sun.

TOP TIP! As well as spraying their droppings, hippos also urinate backward. So, to avoid a smelly shower, never stand behind a hippo!

POO FLINGER

But it gets worse. Male hippos flick their tails around and around as fast as they can when they poo, spreading it far and wide! Experts aren't sure why they do this. It may be to mark their territory (the area of land they control) or to warn other hippos that they are angry and may attack.

Stand back! This hippo is making sure you know he's the boss with a flying poo warning.

YUCK FACTOR!

😫 😫 😫 😫

Poo-spraying, pee-squirting, and gas-belching hippos are no one's idea of polite company.

OPOSSUM

Opossums are smallish, fluffy mammals found in America. They look quite normal—even cute. But when the common opossum is in danger of being attacked or eaten, all that changes! It deliberately makes itself as disgusting as possible, to put potential predators off trying a tasty mouthful.

FOAMING AT THE MOUTH

First, the opossum can use its disgusting drool trick to make attackers think it has a horrible disease. It collects a mouthful of saliva (spit), then blows a mass of bubbling foam from its mouth and nose to make attackers think it is ill or dying. This makes some predators back away.

PLAYING DEAD . . .

For an even better way to repel hunting animals, the opossum "plays dead." It lies still, with its tongue dangling out, and does a poo (as this often happens when animals die). Yuck!

. . . AND NOT EVEN FRESH!

Last of all, the opossum releases a horrible-smelling, greenish slime from its anal glands (two small organs on its rear end). This smells like rotting meat, so that the opossum seems as if it's been dead for several days. When they smell this, most predators decide they're not that hungry after all.

Don't eat me! I'm really not very well. In fact, I'm starting to rot!

DID YOU KNOW?

Opossums can eat several species of poisonous snakes. The poison does not affect them.

JACKAL

Imagine if, when you were hungry and ready for lunch, your mom vomited up some old meat that she'd chewed and swallowed earlier onto your plate—or even right into your mouth! That's how jackals (and several other species) feed their young. It seems REVOLTING to us—but for jackals, it makes a lot of sense.

WHAT HAPPENS?

Jackals leave their puppies in a den, usually a burrow or hollow in the ground, while they hunt for rats, birds, and other prey. Sometimes, instead of hunting, they scavenge by nibbling meat off the carcasses of animals killed by other hunters such as lions.

FEEDING TIME

Then the jackal parents return to their pups with the food in their stomachs. It sounds disgusting, but jackal vomit makes a great baby food. The meat is soft and mushed up—just as humans mush up food for their babies. The pups catch the food from their parents' throats as they vomit it up. This method allows the pups to stay safely in the den, away from danger.

YUCK FACTOR!

We find vomit disgusting, but regurgitating food is the best way for some babies to get food and grow.

MORE REVOLTING REGURGITATORS

Some birds regurgitate food for their babies, too, including vultures, pigeons, and penguins. With penguins, the vomited-up mush is fishy!

Yum! A mother jackal in Kenya gets ready to chew up a rat that she will regurgitate later for her pups.

RAFFLESIA

**Pretty, bright, and delicate, flowers fill your yard with delicious scents.
Except this one! The rafflesia has to be one of the ugliest flowers in the world, as well as being the biggest single bloom on Earth. And on top of that, it smells like rotting meat!**

MMM, SMELL THIS!

Just like other flowers, the rafflesia smells as it does for a good reason—to attract insects to pollinate it. This means spreading pollen from one flower to another, which allows the plant to make seeds. Its stinky, dead-meat whiff attracts flies that like rotten meat, and they end up spreading the pollen around.

FOREST GIANT

This isn't a flower that's going to pop up in your yard overnight. It lives in the steamy rain forests of Southeast Asia, and survives by invading and feeding on another plant, a kind of vine. Its enormous buds and flowers are the only part of the plant you can see. The flower can measure more than 40 inches (1 m) across, and the bud is as big as a football.

The five spotty petals and strange central hole of a rafflesia flower blooming in the rain forest.

YUCK FACTOR!

The revolting rafflesia looks hideous and smells even worse!

TITAN ARUM

The forests of Southeast Asia are home to more than one type of stinky flower. As well as the rafflesia, there's the titan arum, or "corpse lily," which looks completely different from the rafflesia. With a tall central spike surrounded by a trumpetlike shape, it looks like a huge cartoon flower. But it reeks!

TOP TIP! Though the titan arum naturally lives in rain forests, it is often grown in botanical gardens, which are like zoos for plants. When a titan arum is about to bloom, it usually hits the headlines, since they flower very rarely. So look out for news about a titan arum near you, and you could go and see (and smell!) it for yourself.

FLY HEAVEN
Like the rafflesia, the titan arum uses its smell to attract flies to pollinate it. It gives off the smell of rotting flesh and is a dark red color inside so that it looks like meat, too.

WARMING UP
As the titan arum flower blooms, the spike-shaped part gets warm, to make the smell stronger and yuckier!

Tourists gather around a blooming titan arum at Bonn University in Germany.

WHO'S THE BIGGEST? The titan arum is even bigger than the rafflesia, up to 10 feet (3 m) tall. But it's actually made up of lots of tiny flowers, so it doesn't count as the biggest flower in the world.

VENUS FLYTRAP

Plants that eat meat sound like something straight out of a sci-fi movie. But Venus flytraps are real, and they not only eat insects and other animals, they actually grab them and trap them in their spiky-edged "jaws." *Snap!*

Munch! This Venus flytrap has snapped shut on an unsuspecting fly.

HAIR TRIGGER

The Venus flytrap's "traps" are formed from its leaves. Each trap has two halves, like open jaws. Inside, the leaves are covered in tiny hairs. When an insect or other small animal brushes against the hairs, the trap shuts tight. It seals up and forms a kind of "stomach," releasing digestive juices that break the prey down into liquid plant food.

I'M SO HUNGRY!

Most plants don't eat meat, so why do flytraps? They live in North America, in marshy areas where there's plenty of water but very poor soil. They can't get all the nutrients (food chemicals) they need from the soil around them, so they need something extra—in the form of fly-flavored snacks!

TOP TIP! You can buy a Venus flytrap as a houseplant. But don't keep poking it to make the traps shut! It's not good for it.

YUCK FACTOR!

The thought of meat-eating plants is a bit alarming, but Venus flytraps are small and only eat tiny animals.

PITCHER PLANT

There are several types of meat-eating plants, but the pitcher plant is the hungriest of all. It catches its prey using a brilliant booby trap—a deep "pitcher," or jug-shaped container, filled with digestive juices that dissolve any animal that falls inside.

YUCK FACTOR!

A plant that can gobble up a rat is pretty gross!

SLIPPERY RIM

Unlike the Venus flytrap, the pitcher plant doesn't have moving parts that can grab prey. Instead, it attracts passing insects and other animals with sweet-smelling nectar and bright colors. The "pitcher" parts of the plant have very slippery edges. When an animal steps onto them, it slips inside, into a deep vat of deadly liquefying chemicals. The slime around the rim, along with grooves or downward-pointing hairs inside the pitcher, make it almost impossible for trapped animals to climb back out.

MEAT-EATING MONSTERS

Some pitcher plants grow big enough to hold over 5 pints (3 L) of liquid, and can trap and kill animals such as frogs, large spiders, and even mice and rats.

Watch out! If this fly takes one more step, it will fall inside the deadly pitcher.

COULD YOU FALL IN?

There are horror movies that show giant pitcher plants big enough to eat a human—but as far as we know, there are no real pitcher plants that big!

SQUIRTING CUCUMBER

Be careful when you're close to one of these disgusting plants. Even from some distance away, it could squirt you with a jet of slimy, sloppy, jellylike gunk and seeds.

SEED SPREADER

The squirting cucumber is a vinelike plant with hairy, green, oval-shaped fruits. As its fruit grows bigger and riper, pressure builds up inside, until finally— *POP!*—it suddenly breaks off from its stalk, and its slimy insides explode outward. The plant isn't trying to zap you—it does this in order to disperse, or spread, its seeds as far away as possible to give them a chance to grow.

HIGH SPEED SHOOTING

When it first fires from the plant, the cucumber's gloppy gunk can move at an incredible 60 miles per hour (95 km/h) and can fly up to 23 feet (7 m) away. *Splat!*

DID YOU KNOW?

Though it's related to the cucumbers we eat, the squirting cucumber is poisonous, especially if you eat a lot of it. So if any ends up in your mouth, spit it out!

TOP TIP! If you want to set off a ripe squirting cucumber plant, shake it gently— but keep it away from your face.

This plump squirting cucumber fruit will soon splat its seeds and pulp everywhere.

STINKING TOE TREE

Can a tree have toes? Well, the stinking toe tree (also called the West Indian locust) does! Not only does it have parts that look just like a giant's fat, stubby toes—they also smell just like toes! In fact, they smell like the stinkiest feet you've ever smelled or a pile of old, reeking, unwashed socks.

The stinking toe tree's pods contain a delicious, powdery pulp.

YUCK FACTOR!

Just hold your nose, and the yucky stinking toe becomes a tasty morsel.

TOE PODS

The toe tree's "toes" are actually its fruits. They are big, brownish seedpods roughly the size of large potatoes. They grow in clusters, so sometimes they look like a bunch of toes on a foot. Inside each pod is a seed, surrounded by a powdery substance that stinks of cheesy feet. When you crack a seedpod open, the smell goes everywhere!

STINKING TOE SNACK

Amazingly, despite smelling so bad, the inside of the toe fruits is a local delicacy in the Caribbean, where the tree grows. It's said to taste sweet and delicious—but it does give you bad breath!

A stinking toe tree: the place to go for a smelly but satisfying snack.

USEFUL TOE TREE

Hardened sap from the stinking toe tree, known as copal, is used as an incense (burned to release scent) and as a sealant for tooth fillings.

POND SLIME

A pond is an attractive feature of a garden or park—UNLESS it's filled with icky, disgusting pond slime. Green, wet, stringy slime clogs up ponds, blocks out light so other plants can't grow, and looks revolting. And it's especially bad if your friends drag a long, gloppy curtain of slime out of the pond on a stick and flick it at you. Urgh!

YUCK FACTOR!

Pond slime is vile, but it keeps to itself and can't hurt you.

TOP TIP! Gardeners

hate algal slime ruining their ponds. There are chemicals that can kill the algae, but it's often easiest to just fish for the slime with a rake and haul it out.

WHAT IS SLIME?

The slime in ponds (and other still water, such as swamps and canals) looks like a large plant, but it's actually made up of millions and millions of tiny, single-celled living things, called algae.

IN THE CLUB

Some water algae float around on their own. But many species club together in huge groups, or colonies, making what looks like long strand, blanket, or mat shapes. The individual cells are held together by sticky slime, and that's what makes pond slime so gloppy and revolting.

SLIME INVASION!

Living together in groups seems to help algae grow and multiply faster. They can soon completely take over a pond.

Keep that away from me! Green, gloppy, soaking wet pond slime looks and feels disgusting.

SLIME MOLD

Overnight, a weird, jellylike blob appears on your lawn. It seems like something from a sci-fi movie. In the past, people thought these bizarre blobs really did come from space—they are sometimes called "star jelly"—and they have even been used as evidence for UFO landings. The truth is a bit less exciting (though still disgusting). In fact, these are creatures called slime molds.

Slime blobs in nature inspired the Blob *movies, which feature an alien slimeball.*

A MASS OF CELLS

A slime mold is not an animal or plant—it's actually made up of single-celled creatures called amoebae. For part of their lives, each amoeba lives on its own. But at one stage, they join together to make a massive supercell that looks like a slimy, stringy bag of jelly.

ONE MIND

Even weirder, when they are joined together, the cells can act like one single living creature. They work together to make the whole mass of jelly crawl forward, so that it can move around on plant matter to feed.

Not a jelly from space, but a species called red raspberry slime mold.

SUPER SLIME

If you cut a slime mold in half, it makes two slime molds. Two can also join together to make one bigger one.

TOP TIP! If you don't want a slime mold around, you can simply wash it away with a garden hose.

YUCK FACTOR!

A blob of jelly with a mind of its own—the ultimate slime!

DISGUSTING RED FUNGUS

A disgusting red fungus can have up to 16 slimy tentacles.

You might see a mushroom growing in your yard from time to time, but you probably don't expect it to look like this! This freaky fungus, with its alien-looking red tentacles smeared with revolting-smelling brown slime, has the scientific name *Aseroë rubra*—which literally means "disgusting red."

TOP TIP! Don't touch or eat this yucky fungus, and keep pets away from it, too. It's poisonous, and some dogs have died after eating it.

YUCK FACTOR!

Stinky, slimy, and ugly, this has to be the world's yuckiest mushroom.

SLIMY SPORES

Like some stinky species of plants, this disgusting red fungus smells like rotting meat in order to attract flies. When they land on the fungus, the black slime, which contains tiny spores (the fungus version of seeds), sticks to their feet and bodies. So, as the flies move around, they spread the spores and new fungi grow.

A STARFISH—OR A GORY WOUND?

This fungus is sometimes called the starfish or sea anemone fungus because of its starlike shape and red color. Some experts think it looks the way it does to make flies think it's a rotting wound in the side of an animal's body— since that's where some types of flies like to lay their eggs.

HITCHING A RIDE

This disgusting red fungus is found in Australia and the Pacific Islands, but its spores sometimes escape, often in potted plants. So it can pop up anywhere in the world.

STINKHORN

The name "stinkhorn" tells you a little bit about this disgusting mushroom. It has a long, white stalk with an oval, greenish cap on top, dripping with stinky, spore-filled slime. Like the disgusting red fungus, it reeks of rotten flesh—or sometimes smelly animal poo—to attract flies to land on it, helping to spread its spores.

SPOTTING A STINKHORN

Stinkhorns grow in Europe and North America, usually in forests or yards. You may smell one before you see it—it's a revolting, sickly-sweet smell that can make you feel ill. Then look out for the stinkhorn's tall white stalk and flies buzzing around its tip.

WITCHES' EGG

You might also see a stinkhorn "egg"! When the fungus first appears from underground, it's inside a pale, egglike ball from which it then bursts out. Though not real eggs, these used to be called "witches' eggs," perhaps because they appeared mysteriously from the ground.

Flies love the rotting, pooey smell of stinkhorn!

STINKY, BUT EDIBLE
Though it's smelly and slimy, the stinkhorn isn't poisonous, and some people eat the "eggs." The fungus has been used as a folk remedy to treat many illnesses, from aching joints to cancer!

YUCK FACTOR!

A disgusting fungus, but it has its uses and admirers.

HEAD LOUSE

Ugh! Out of all the disgusting creatures in this book, the head louse is probably one you've been closest to. Head lice spend their whole lives on human heads—very often children's heads. They feed by biting your scalp and sucking your blood—which makes you incredibly itchy. In fact, you're probably feeling itchy just thinking about it. . . .

Head louse eggs, or nits, glued to human hair.

DID YOU KNOW?
Scientists have found that head lice prefer to live in girls' hair!

NITS!
Nits are head lice eggs. The female lays each egg close to a hair root, using a special glue to stick it to the hair. As soon as the larva (baby) hatches, it starts biting you and sucking your blood. When they bite, lice inject a chemical into your blood to stop it from clotting and scabbing over. Then they slurp it up!

STUCK ON YOU
Head lice can't fly, jump, or even walk very well—their curled feet are designed for holding onto hairs. So they're happy to stay on your head, laying eggs that hatch into new lice. They only spread to another person if your heads brush together, and they can wriggle onto the other person's hair.

YUCK FACTOR!
😖 😖
They're not nice, but many of us have had head lice—and survived

TOP TIP! It's easy to get rid of head lice by combing them out carefully and washing your hair with special head lice shampoo.

EYELASH MITE

Imagine a tiny, wriggly creepy-crawly living in the roots of your eyelashes. How gross is that?! Well, it may be gross, but you probably have quite a few wriggling around among your eyelashes right now. Many children, and more than half of adults, have eyelash mites.

WHAT ARE THEY?

Mites are related to spiders, though eyelash mites actually have a wormlike shape, with eight tiny legs at one end. They live around the base of the eyelashes, rooted in the hair follicle (the hole that the eyelash grows from). But they can come out and creep around, especially at night. They can also be found on other hairs on the face, such as eyebrow hairs. They eat dead skin and sebum, the oily stuff that makes your hair greasy if you don't wash it.

WHY CAN'T I SEE THEM?

These mites are teeny-tiny—less than 1/50 of an inch (1/2 mm) long. You won't be able to see them by looking in a mirror. But you might spot some if you collect one of your own eyelashes after it falls out and look at it under a microscope.

YUCK FACTOR!

Eyelash mites are revolting if you think about them too much—but they're pretty harmless.

TOP TIP! It's very difficult to get rid of eyelash mites, and even if you do, they just come back. So don't worry about them!

This is an eyelash mite, magnified. The mite's rear end anchors itself in the hair follicle.

YOU'LL GET THEM

The older you get, the more likely you are to have eyelash mites. They spread from one person to another when people's faces touch.

TICK

You're walking in a forest when you notice something small and round stuck to your leg. A tick! Like mosquitoes, lice, and lots of other creepy-crawlies, ticks like to bite you and suck your blood. What's especially disgusting is the way they attach themselves to your skin and hang on while their bodies slowly fill with blood.

TOP TIP! To get a tick off you, pull it gently using tweezers or a special tick remover to hold its head. DON'T squeeze its body or burn it—these things can make matters worse.

YUCK FACTOR!

There's something deeply disgusting about the way a tick clings on and fills up as it feeds.

HOW A TICK FINDS YOU

Ticks don't live on their hosts all the time—they live in long grass or on trees, and brush onto your body as you go past. They also feed on other animals, such as dogs and deer. Some ticks can detect the warmth of your body or the gases in your breath, then creep and crawl onto you.

DID YOU KNOW?

Ticks can give you several diseases, including Lyme disease, which causes terrible tiredness and headaches.

FILLING STATION

Next, the tick finds some bare skin and burrows its sharp mouthparts, and most of its head, into your flesh. It can hang on for minutes, hours, or even days as it drinks its fill.

This tick is growing fat and swollen as it fills with human blood.

FLEA

A flea uses its massive back legs to jump up to 200 times its body length.

BOINGGG! Unlike some parasites (creatures that live in or on bigger creatures), you're quite likely to see a flea as it leaps from one person to another, or from your pet onto you, with the superhuman jumping strength of its powerful back legs. These wingless insects are among the most irritating of parasites, since their bites make you ITCH badly.

EGGS EVERYWHERE

Fleas hop around on people and animals, but they also make their homes in your carpets, beds, and furniture, and in dog and cat beds. Their eggs collect in dusty corners and bedding, and when they hatch, the larvae eat dead skin and crumbs. Only as adults do they hop onto you for a blood meal. This makes fleas horribly hard to get rid of, as you have to de-flea your whole house.

ITCHY SPOTS

When a flea bites, it injects its saliva into you, and this causes horrible itching and a red, sore spot. It can give some people an allergic rash as well.

YUCK FACTOR!

Fleas can cause serious problems, but they're mainly more annoying than disgusting.

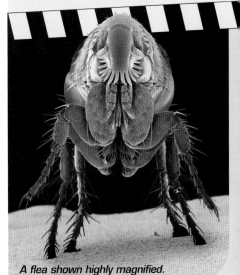

A flea shown highly magnified.

LEECH

You're paddling in a stream when—ugh!—a slimy, wriggly creature clamps itself onto you—and starts sucking your blood. It's a leech, a kind of legless, boneless animal related to worms.

BLOODSUCKERS

Leeches have a sucker that clamps fast to your skin. Then they use either a needlelike mouth or a set of sharp teeth to cut your skin. They suck your blood until they're full (this can take 20 minutes!), then drop off. However, not all leeches are out to get you. Of over 600 species, only a few feed on human blood. The rest eat other creatures such as water worms.

Because leeches release an anesthetic when they attach, you won't feel the biting leech until you brush over it.

BLOODLETTING

In medieval times, people thought illnesses could be caused by having too much blood. So they stuck leeches onto themselves on purpose, to suck some out. Some doctors still use leeches today, though for different reasons (see page 111).

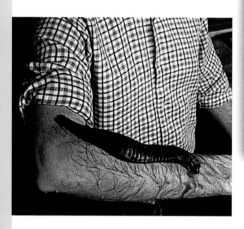

Leeches range from tiny critters just a half inch (1 cm) long to monsters such as the giant Amazonian leech, which can be over 12 inches (30 cm) long.

TOP TIP! The best way to remove a leech is to slide a fingernail under its side gently, to break the sucker seal. DON'T squeeze the leech, burn it, or stab it! This could make it vomit its stomach contents into your bloodstream, giving you nasty germs.

MOSQUITO

The mosquito is probably the most famous bloodsucking animal of all. These spindly flies cause horribly itchy spots when they bite you. Even worse, they spread seriously deadly diseases including malaria and yellow fever.

NEEDLE NOSE

If you watch a mosquito up close while it's snacking on you, you'll see it has jabbed your skin with a very long, needlelike mouthpart, called a proboscis. This sticks into your skin and injects chemicals that stop blood from clotting. Then the mosquito uses its mouth as a straw to suck up the blood. As it does, you can see its transparent body bulging and turning red with its big blood meal.

YUCK FACTOR!

Mosquitoes can be very dangerous but only moderately disgusting.

BLOODTHIRSTY BEASTS?

Surprisingly, mosquitoes actually don't need to suck our blood very much at all. The larvae (young) feed on plankton, and the adults usually feed on nectar and fruit. Only female mosquitoes suck blood—they do it to get nutrients they need for laying eggs.

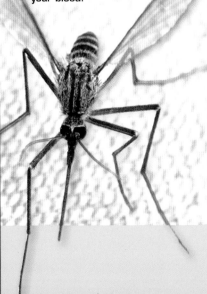

The mosquito uses its needlelike proboscis to stab through your skin and suck up your blood.

TOP TIP! You can save yourself from bites by sleeping under a mosquito net and using bug repellent on your skin. In countries where malaria is common, you can take special anti-malarial tablets, too.

BEDBUG

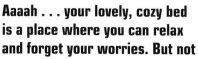

Aaaah . . . your lovely, cozy bed
is a place where you can relax
and forget your worries. But not
if it's infested with creepy, biting bedbugs! These yucky little
beasts like to bite you in the night while you're asleep, leaving you
itching, scratching, tossing, and turning.

TOP TIP! You can catch
bedbugs by shining a flashlight
on your bed in the middle of
the night, and then sweeping
them up before they have time
to run. However, complete
"debugging" involves thorough
searching and cleaning. Some
infestations may call for
professional bug killers!

HIDING AWAY

Bedbugs live in beds, but they can
be hard to find. They hate light and
disappear during the day. They are
small and very flat, and can hide in
mattress seams and tiny cracks.
They have even been known to hide
on the ceiling above a bed, then drop
down onto you when you're asleep.
Aarrggh! Luckily, though, most
homes these days don't have them.

FEEDING TIME!

Once it's really dark and you're
lying nice and still, the bedbugs
start to nibble. They jab you with
sharp, beaklike mouthparts that
have two tubes in them—one for
injecting painkilling chemicals, the
other for sucking blood. You don't
feel it at first, but later you get a
horribly itchy bump.

*Creepy bedbugs bite humans when they
are at their most vulnerable: when they
are asleep!*

THREE IN A ROW

Bedbugs often leave three bites in a nice neat row—probably
because they have to let go and reattach themselves when you
move. These three-bite patterns are sometimes called
"breakfast, lunch, and dinner"!

DUST MITE

You may be able to avoid bedbugs—but you almost certainly do have dust mites in your home and in your bed. In fact, most beds, as well as carpets and sofas, are home to thousands of these teeny, spiderlike creatures! They get their name because they feed on dead skin flakes, which are often found in household dust.

YUCK FACTOR!

It is revolting to think about how many creepy-crawlies we live with. It's a good thing these are too small to see!

TOP TIP! You can kill dust mites and get rid of their poo by washing your bedclothes at 140°F (60°C). But they'll still be in the mattress, so it's hard to get rid of them completely.

MINI MITES

The amount of skin that flakes off our bodies every day is tiny—but so are dust mites. Each blind, eight-legged mite is less than 1/50 of an inch (1/2 mm) long. Each human sheds enough skin to keep several thousand mites well fed.

MUNCH, MUNCH

As dust mites munch their way through dust and skin bits, they leave droppings, as well as their own skins, which they shed like a snake does. These substances can cause serious allergies in some people, giving them asthma or a rash.

A microscopic view of a dust mite— a big fan of dead skin for dinner.

DID YOU KNOW?

A human sheds millions of dead skin cells every day—adding up to about 2 pounds (1 kg) of skin every year.

TAPEWORM

Has anyone ever said "you must have a tapeworm!" because you're very hungry and eat a lot? It's usually meant as a joke, but tapeworms are real, and they can make you feel hungry—by living in your intestines and eating your food.

YUCK FACTOR!

😝 😝 😝 😝

Being home to a parasite this big is a really repulsive idea.

SWALLOWING A CYST

A tapeworm larva (or baby) is called a cyst. They are sometimes found in dirty water or undercooked food. If you swallow one, it grows into an adult tapeworm inside you. As its name suggests, it's tape-shaped, with little hooks on its head to fix itself firmly to the inside of your intestine.

DID YOU KNOW?

Some tapeworms can grow to a shocking 27 feet (8 m) long while living inside you. How revolting!

EGGS

Tapeworms lay eggs that come out of your bottom when you use the toilet. In countries with poor sewage systems, dirty water from toilets can get into water that's used for drinking or for washing food, so tapeworms can spread easily. You can also catch one from eating raw meat from an animal, such as a pig, that has a tapeworm itself.

This tapeworm was living inside a pet cat! Yuck!

TOP TIP! To avoid tapeworms, always wash your hands before eating, and steer clear of undercooked meat and fish.

ROUNDWORM

Roundworms are the worms that cats, dogs, and humans have when we say they've "got worms." These worms are smaller than tapeworms—from less than 1/2 inch (1 cm) to over 10 inches (25 cm) long. But that doesn't make them any less disgusting!

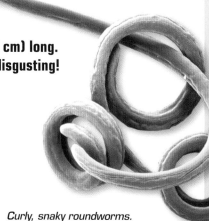

CATCHING WORMS

People catch worms by swallowing worm eggs found in dirty water, food, or soil, or on their hands. Inside you, the eggs hatch into worms that live in your intestines. Threadworms, very small worms, eventually die and come out in the toilet. Some bigger roundworms, though, can cause more trouble.

Curly, snaky roundworms.

WRIGGLY INVASION

If you have a bad case of worms and don't get it fixed, the worms can move to other parts of your body, or multiply, so that you end up with a big mass of worms inside you—called a "heavy worm burden." Ugh! Even worse, a worm could come out of your nose or eye, or you could vomit up worms.

YUCK FACTOR!

The possibility of a worm coming out of your eye gives this disgusting creepy-crawly top marks.

TOP TIP! Always wash your hands well after using the toilet or changing a baby's diaper to make sure worms can't spread.

DON'T PANIC!
Doctors can get rid of worms quickly with medicine. Problems only happen when the worms aren't treated.

GUINEA WORM

Imagine having to spend a month slowly pulling a 3-foot (1 m) worm out of your skin! That's what happens if your body gets invaded by a Guinea worm. And not only is it gross, it's horribly painful, too.

WHAT'S IN THE WATER?

Before infecting humans, Guinea worm larvae (young) live inside tiny water animals called copepods that live in dirty, stagnant (non-flowing) water. When you drink the water, the copepods die in your stomach, but the Guinea worm larvae grow into adult worms.

GET ME OUT OF HERE!

Inside you, a female worm can grow for as long as a year. Eventually, she needs to emerge from your body to lay eggs, so she makes her way to your skin, where a nasty blister forms. You know you have a Guinea worm problem when you see one end of the worm sticking out! Yuck!

TOP TIP! To get rid of a Guinea worm, you have to wind it very gently around a pencil or twig, pulling a little more out each day. This can take weeks, and causes an agonizing, burning pain.

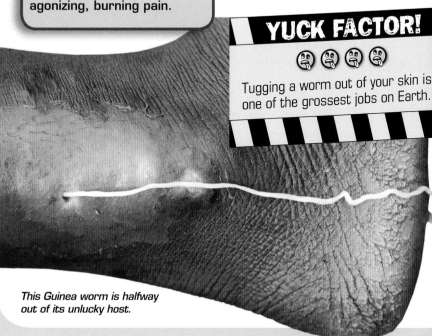

YUCK FACTOR!

Tugging a worm out of your skin is one of the grossest jobs on Earth.

This Guinea worm is halfway out of its unlucky host.

TONGUE-EATING LOUSE

What if a sneaky parasite ate your entire tongue and then lived in your mouth acting as a replacement? You would have a tongue-sized bug living there forever! That's what happens to snapper fish when the tongue-eating louse finds them.

MMM! TASTY TONGUE!

The 1.5-inch (4 cm) louse, which looks a bit like a wood louse, invades the fish by swimming in through its gills. It attaches itself to the fish's tongue and sucks blood from it until the tongue drops off. Then the louse clings to the muscles at the base of the tongue, and becomes a new tongue for the fish! It feeds on the fish's blood and body fluids.

COULD IT HAPPEN TO US?

Don't worry about a louse invasion when you're in the ocean. The tongue-eating louse needs gills to swim in through—and humans don't have gills. And it mainly invades one type of fish, the spotted rose snapper.

Open wide! A look inside this fish's mouth shows a sneaky tongue-eating louse.

YUCK FACTOR!

It's weird, but not all that revolting—and it can't harm us.

SUPERMARKET SURPRISE

In 2005, a shopper in England bought a whole snapper fish to cook and eat, and was amazed to find a fully grown, fat tongue-eating louse inside its mouth.

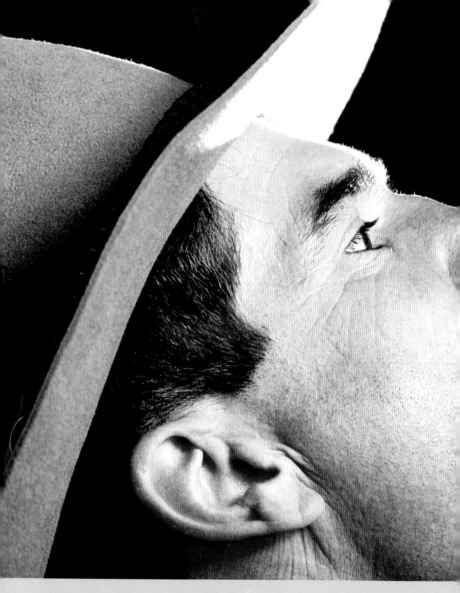

DISGUSTING

We humans might like to think of ourselves as clean and sweet-smelling, but that's far from the truth! Our bodies produce disgusting things—and to get rid of them, we've come up with several revolting

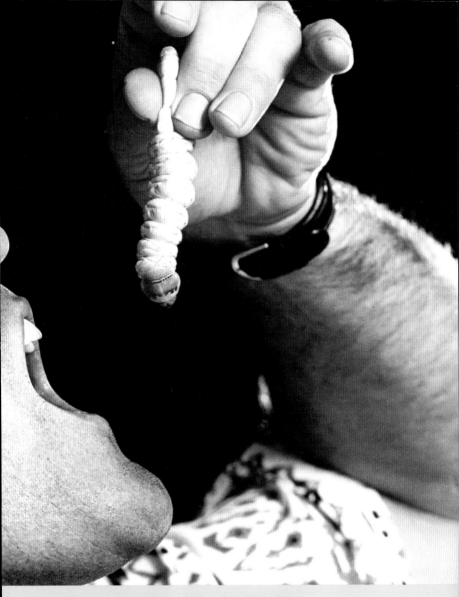

HUMANS

inventions! Many of us also eat food that other people find deeply vile, including rotten fish, maggot-filled cheese, bird spit, animal poo, and crispy roasted tarantulas.

GERMS IN CHEESE

If you were invited to eat a delicacy made of curdled, month-old milk that smelled, grew crust, and was injected with greenish blue mold, you might think "Yuck! No thanks!" Yet you have probably eaten all kinds of cheese without a thought.

Mold is added to give blue cheese a tangy flavor that some people love.

IS CHEESE DISGUSTING?

If you're used to cheese, it probably seems very normal and not disgusting at all. But in some places, especially parts of Asia, people aren't used to eating dairy products, and their bodies are not good at digesting milk and cheese. They often find the idea of cheese quite disgusting, especially moldy blue cheese! Cheese is made of milk that has been allowed to go bad, but in a carefully controlled way. The strong smells and flavors of cheese come partly from bacteria that is added to help milk change into cheese.

MOLDY VEINS

To make blue cheese, something even more disgusting happens. It has mold spores injected or stirred into it to make clumps and streaks (or "veins") of mold grow. When we find mold on bread or bananas, we throw them away— yet we eat it in cheese! It adds a sharp, tangy taste and makes cheese smell like sweaty socks.

Bacterial gas is what makes Swiss cheese so holey.

DID YOU KNOW?

The holes in Swiss cheese are made by gas bubbles that are released by bacteria in the cheese.

MAGGOT CHEESE

Some cheeses are more disgusting than others, and maggot cheese from Italy, or casu marzu, is probably the most disgusting of all. It's rotten, stinking, and crawling with live maggots! Gross!

AGAINST THE LAW

Maggot cheese is actually banned in the parts of Italy where it is popular, but people still eat it. They take normal cheese and let insects called cheese flies lay their eggs in it. The eggs hatch into maggots that feed on the cheese, making it rotten, runny, and very strong-tasting.

Casu marzu cheese writhing with live maggots. Imagine this on a cracker!

WOULD YOU LIKE MAGGOTS WITH THAT?

Some people eat the wriggly maggots along with the cheese. Others seal the cheese in a container first so that the maggots can't breathe, and they jump out of the cheese and die.

MIND YOUR EYES!

The maggots can coil their bodies up and then spring up to 6 inches (15 cm) into the air. So while eating, people shield their eyes with their hands to keep leaping maggots out. Lovely!

TOP TIP! When eating maggot cheese, check to see if the maggots are still wriggling and jumping. If they're not, it means they're dead, and the cheese is considered to have gone bad, which means it can't be eaten.

GUGA

Guga is the name of a delicacy eaten on the Isle of Lewis, off the coast of Scotland. It is the meat of baby gannets, a type of seabird. Since gannets feed on fish, their meat tastes and smells very fishy, salty, and strong.

FIRST, CATCH YOUR GANNET

Though many people find its taste revolting and its smell even worse, guga is a highly prized specialty since it is so rare and hard to catch. Every autumn, a boat leaves the Isle of Lewis carrying guga hunters 40 miles (65 km) north to a rock in the sea named Sula Sgeir (meaning "gannet rock"), where gannets nest. The hunters catch the young gannets using loops on the ends of long poles. They have been hunting the gannets in this traditional way for hundreds of years.

YUCK FACTOR!

Though guga seems vile, many people love it—though everyone agrees that it really smells gross while it's being cooked.

Young gannets cannot fly, making them easier for guga hunters to catch.

DID YOU KNOW?

The gannet is a protected species, but special rules allow guga hunting once a year. However, some animal rights campaigners are trying to get guga hunting stopped.

Sula Sgeir looms in the mist as an adult gannet soars in the wind, hunting for fish.

TOP TIP! To cook guga, you have to first scrub off the grease and salt, then boil it several times. The greasy fat needs to be skimmed off each time.

HÁKARL

Hákarl is poisonous, dried, rotted shark meat. Delicious! It's eaten in Iceland, where it's a traditional dish, though it tastes so horrible that even there many people don't like it. Like some other disgusting foods, it smells even worse than it tastes.

SMELLY SHARKS

Hákarl is made from either Greenland sharks or basking sharks. Their meat contains very smelly, harmful chemicals. To make it edible, the dead shark has to be pressed and squeezed, traditionally by burying it under a pile of stones for several weeks. After it has begun to rot, the shark meat is hung to dry for another two months, then cut into small cubes.

YUCK FACTOR!

Hákarl is regularly described as one of the most disgusting-smelling foods in the world.

TOP TIP! When you have hákarl for the first time, try holding your nose so that the horrendous smell doesn't put you off before you begin.

WHAT'S IT LIKE?

Even those who like hákarl have to wash it down with a strong-tasting drink to make it bearable! It is said to taste very sharp, smelling strongly of ammonia, a chemical that can make your eyes water. Its texture is soft and squishy, like meat fat.

An Icelandic farmer hangs shark meat to dry in his shed as part of the process of making hákarl.

CHINESE CATERPILLAR FUNGUS

A handful of freshly picked caterpillar mushrooms.

In the Himalayas where it is found, this strange fungus is called "yartsa gunbu" or "dong chong xia cao." These names mean "winter worm, summer grass." In other words, something that starts life as a caterpillar later becomes a plant (or, in this case, a mushroom).

YUCK FACTOR!

This caterpillar-mushroom combo is enough to put anyone off—especially if you don't like mushrooms to start with!

TOP TIP! People can eat caterpillar mushrooms whole or crumble them into soup. They are also made into pills. But if you should be offered one, it's best not to eat it, since they have been known to make people ill.

CATERPILLAR INVASION

What actually happens is that a fungus invades the ghost moth caterpillar, which lives underground in the winter. The fungus spreads its roots through the caterpillar's whole body, killing and preserving it. The caterpillar dies just under the soil's surface. In the spring, a mushroom sprouts out of its head! When you pick the mushroom, the hardened, dead caterpillar is still attached.

MUSHROOM MEDICINE

Caterpillar mushrooms have been eaten for centuries by mountain people, and they are used as a traditional medicine in China. Scientists have found that they contain useful medical chemicals.

This man is digging for caterpillar fungus, which is very valuable in China.

EYEBALLS

Maybe you've eaten eyeballs made of jelly or chocolate at Halloween. But a lot of people like eating REAL eyeballs—especially those from cows, sheep, and fish.

Some people love to munch eyeballs just like this one. Imagine biting into it!

ROASTED SHEEP'S EYE

Sheep eyeballs are popular in Saudi Arabia, where people often roast a whole sheep for a feast. The roasted eyeballs are usually plucked out and eaten first. They are said to be very chewy and squishy to eat. Yummm!

FISH EYES

In many parts of Asia, the eyes are considered the tastiest parts of a fish. You can pop or scoop the eyeballs out of the fish's head and eat them whole. Many people spit out the hard cornea, the front part of the eye.

STUFFED EYEBALLS

For a traditional French recipe called "yeux de veau farcis," you boil calves' eyeballs, cut off the cornea, lens, and iris, stuff each eyeball with chopped mushrooms, then fry them in bread crumbs.

TOP TIP! If you ever have to eat an eyeball when you don't really want to, gulp it down whole. Chewing releases the gooey jelly inside!

ESPECIALLY FOR YOU

Eyes are only a small part of an animal, so you don't normally have a big plateful of them. They are treated as a special snack or treat, or given to the guest of honor at a dinner party.

DURIAN

YUCK FACTOR!

It smells baaaaad, but apart from that it's quite lovely.

Durian isn't a scary animal body part or a delicacy made from rotted food—it's just a fruit. What could be so disgusting about that? Well, the durian is famous for its revolting smell, though some people love it.

WHAT IS IT?

Durians grow on trees found in Southeast Asian countries such as Indonesia and Malaysia. The fruits can grow up to the size of footballs, and are covered in spikes. Inside are large seeds surrounded by creamy, custardy flesh.

A durian cut open to reveal its soft, ripe, stinky flesh.

AN INDESCRIBABLE EXPERIENCE

The smell of the durian has been compared to many things, including vomit, smelly cheese, dirty socks, rotten onions, cat pee, antiseptic, toilets, pig poo, and cream cheese! Yet, although it smells bad, many people adore the taste of durians and will pay lots of money for a ripe one. It is said to taste buttery, custardy, nutty, and fruity.

DID YOU KNOW?

In Thailand, it is illegal to eat durians in public because the smell could upset other people.

Durians grow on trees up to 120 feet (36 m) tall, which are native to Brunei, Indonesia, and Malaysia.

No smoking · Fine $1000

No eating and drinking · Fine $500

No flammable goods · Fine $5000

No durians

A railway sign in Singapore: No durians allowed.

TOP TIP! Do not hang around under a durian tree! The heavy fruits can kill people when they ripen and fall.

CIVET COFFEE

The palm civet is a shy, nocturnal creature that is rarely seen.

YUCK FACTOR!

Civet-poo coffee isn't actually poo, so it's not all that disgusting!

It's the most expensive and prized coffee in the world, and it comes from . . . an animal's poo! The coffee is called "kopi luwak," meaning "civet coffee," and it's made using coffee beans that have passed through the intestines of a Southeast Asian animal called the civet cat.

COFFEE BERRIES

Coffee beans grow inside fruits called coffee berries, which are eaten by the civet cats. Their bodies digest the soft fruit, but the harder beans stay intact. The beans are collected from the civet cat's dung, washed, and roasted, ready to be ground and made into coffee. It can cost over $160 per pound, or as much as $80 for a cup in a café.

IS IT WORTH IT?

Civet coffee is said to taste extremely smooth, chocolaty, rich, and delicious. There are two reasons for this. Firstly, the civet cats like eating the ripest, most perfect berries, which contain the best beans. Secondly, chemicals in the animals' intestines soak into the beans, softening them and changing their flavor.

WHAT ABOUT GERMS?

Although it's fished out of animal droppings, the coffee is roasted at a high temperature so any germs are killed. It's completely safe to drink.

You can clearly see the coffee beans in these civet droppings.

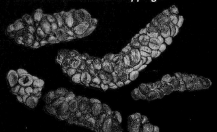

ANIMAL FEET

Feet may not seem like they have much meat, but they have actually been a favorite, cheap food for centuries. They just have to be carefully cooked to make them less chewy and bony.

BIRD FEET

In many parts of Asia you can buy a chicken or duck foot on the street as a snack, just like a hot dog. The feet are stewed or boiled for a long time so that their tough, stringy tendons and joints turn into a chewy, gooey jelly. They are still full of tiny bones, though, which you have to spit out. Some people also make bird feet into soups and stews.

Get your takeout here! A box of fried chicken feet makes a nice chewy snack.

ELEPHANT'S FOOT

In 1790, a French explorer named François Le Vaillant described how he was served elephant's foot in Africa as a meal! His hosts buried the feet in hot embers from a fire, baking them until they were soft. "It looked so nice," he explained, "and exhaled so delicious an odor, that I was impatient to taste it. It was a breakfast for a king!"

TASTY TROTTERS

Pig's feet, or trotters, have a bit more meat on them. In China, they're made into a spicy stew, and in Sri Lanka you can get pig's-trotter curry. In Italy, they take the bones out of pig's trotters and stuff them to make a kind of foot sausage.

BIRD'S NEST SOUP

It's disgusting enough to think of a soup made of nests. But the ones in bird's nest soup aren't made of twigs and grass like most birds' nests. No—they're made of bird spit!

SALIVA SOUP

Bird's nest soup is made from the nests of small Southeast Asian birds called swiftlets. They make their nests high on the walls of sea caves, gluing bits of moss, hair, feathers, and seaweed to the cave wall with strands of sticky saliva. It hardens to form a small cup shape. Collectors climb inside the caves to reach the nests. In Indonesia, there are also artificial caves built for the swiftlets to nest in.

YUCK FACTOR!

Gluey, boiled bird spit—yuck!

Bird's nest soup in a restaurant, ready to eat.

CHINESE DELICACY

The nests are shipped to China, where they are in great demand to make bird's nest soup. When boiled in water, the saliva swells and dissolves, making a gelatinous goop, which is usually mixed with chicken for extra flavor.

A bird's nest collector examines his latest find inside a cave in Thailand.

The inside of a swiftlet nest, still slightly moist with spit.

DID YOU KNOW?

Swiftlets' nests are among the most pricey foods on Earth— 1 pound (0.5 kg) of the nests can cost more than $1,200.

TOP TIP! It's best to avoid bird's nest soup, since harvesting the nests can destroy the swiftlets' eggs and reduce their numbers.

CHOCOLATE-COVERED ANTS

You really can buy chocolate-covered ants—mainly as a novelty food. But in South America, Africa, and Asia, eating ants is widespread. They play an important role in many people's diets.

GIANT TOASTED ANTS
in chocolate coating

Tasty ants, toasted and ready to eat: This is what a packet of ants might look like!

CATCHING ANTS

People use all kinds of tricks to harvest ants. In Thailand, people dig up anthills or knock ant swarms off trees, then dunk the ants in water to separate them from their eggs and bits of soil. In parts of Brazil, people stand hollow twigs filled with oil in the ground to attract ants. Then they pick up the twigs and slurp the ants off.

ANT RECIPES

Some ants can be gobbled up raw, but they are usually cooked. As well as being coated in chocolate, ants can be stir-fried or made into soups, pâtés, or burgers. In Mexico, people also eat ant eggs and larvae (babies). Different species have different flavors, but they can taste like bacon, butter, or lemons!

DID YOU KNOW?

There are thought to be more ants on Earth than any other animal or insect. All of the ants in the world combined weigh as much as all the humans in the world—maybe even more!

TOP TIP! Cooking some poisonous ants by boiling them or frying them gets rid of the chemicals in their stings.

MOTHBURGER

Mmm—a traditional mothburger recipe! First, go to the caves where bogong moths gather to roost in the thousands every summer (you'll find them in Australia's Snowy Mountains). Then scoop up handfuls of tasty moths and roll them in hot ashes to burn off their wings and legs. Mash them up to make delicious "moth meat." Shape it into a ball, squash it to make a burger, and roast it over a campfire. Yum!

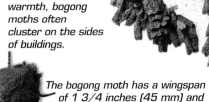

Attracted by warmth, bogong moths often cluster on the sides of buildings.

The bogong moth has a wingspan of 1 3/4 inches (45 mm) and two spots on each wing.

YUCK FACTOR!

Would you like moths mashed, rolled into a ball, and served on a bun at your next barbecue? Maybe not.

MOTH FEAST

Mothburgers were traditionally eaten by Australian Aboriginal (native) people at a special summer festival. The moths make a very good source of food and energy, since they contain a lot of fat and protein. So it made sense to use them when they were so plentiful.

TOP TIP! If you're not very hungry, you don't have to eat a whole mothburger. Another traditional way is to enjoy the moths one by one, as a snack.

SUMMER SNACK

Today, the moths are not an important part of most Australians' diets. But since so many moths arrive each year, they are an important food for all kinds of other animals, such as spiders, lizards, and mountain pygmy possums. You can still try them at the Ngan Girra Festival, which is held in New South Wales, Australia, every summer.

Collect your moths from caves and follow the recipe. . . .

WITCHETTY GRUBS

Plump, juicy witchetty grubs.

Witchetty grubs are big, fat, creamy white, wriggly baby insects that have been a traditional snack in Australia for thousands of years. They are one of the most famous insect foods in the world.

GRUB GRUB

"Grub" is another name for a larva, or baby insect. Witchetty grubs are a type of moth larvae, so they're really a kind of caterpillar. The larvae can grow to 2.8 inches (7 cm) long, and you can eat them raw, fry them, roast them, or cook them in the hot ashes of a campfire. They taste like nutty, buttery scrambled eggs.

DESERT SNACK

In the past, witchetty grubs were an important food for Aboriginal (native) people living in the outback (Australian desert). They would dig up the grubs from underground, where they live inside the roots and trunks of certain types of trees and bushes, most often the river red gum tree, which is native to Australia. Today, not many people rely on them for food, but you can still eat them at some restaurants and festivals.

YUCK FACTOR!

They may seem disgusting at first, but they're delicious.

These witchetty grubs are being prepared for cooking.

TOP TIP! Witchetty grubs make a great barbecue food. You cook them on a skewer, just like a kebab.

FRIED GRASSHOPPERS

Boing! Grasshoppers and their hopping cousins, crickets, cicadas, and locusts, are among the best insect foods in the world. They are large, packed with protein, and tasty, and there are millions of them!

If you're nervous about tasting insects, try them chocolate-dipped.

EVERYDAY SNACK
Across Asia, and in parts of the Americas and Africa, grasshoppers and locusts are a common food. They are usually fried or roasted with salt, and are eaten as a snack along with a drink. In Australia, you can even buy a locust recipe book, which calls them "sky prawns"!

ANCIENT HISTORY
People have been eating bouncing bugs for thousands of years. The ancient Greek philosopher Aristotle liked eating cicadas!

YUCK FACTOR!

If you have to eat an insect, a grasshopper is probably your best bet. Just imagine it's a shrimp!

TOP TIP! Before eating grasshoppers, it's best to take off their large wings and legs.

A pile of large fried grasshoppers like this will fill you up with healthy protein.

FOOD IN A FAMINE
Swarms of locusts often cause food shortages by eating farmers' crops. But people may be able to survive by just eating the locusts instead. In fact, experts think insects of all kinds will become a more important food in the future, as climate change causes crop failures and famines.

MOPANE WORMS

A mopane worm is a type of caterpillar that lives in trees.

Chewy, meaty mopane worms are a staple food all over southern Africa. Once you've squeezed out the slimy green guts (yuck!), you can have them as a snack with a cream cheese dip or in a hearty stew.

YUCK FACTOR!

Their slimy insides aren't nice, but these are a very normal food for millions of people.

TOP TIP! Before eating a mopane worm, you have to get rid of its bitter-tasting innards. You do this by squeezing it like a tube of toothpaste, then shaking it to flick the green slime away.

CATERPILLAR SEASON

Mopane worms aren't actually worms, but a type of moth caterpillar. They hatch in early summer (November in southern Africa) and crawl all over mopane trees, feeding and growing fat. People gather them, then dry them in the sun. They are also canned and sold in supermarkets. In fact, mopane worms are such an important food that during worm season, sales of other meat drop dramatically.

WHAT DO THEY TASTE LIKE?

Some say mopane worms don't taste like much at all, so they're often added to a spicy tomato stew to give them more flavor. But, fried or barbecued, some people think they taste like roast chicken.

Mopane worms are being cooked over an open fire here, ready for a feast.

ROASTED SPIDERS

For those who are scared to even go near a spider, this is probably the most revolting creepy-crawly snack of all. Especially because if you're going to bother cooking and eating spiders, it makes sense to choose the biggest, fattest ones. . . .

READY TO ROAST

Spiders are most popular as a food in South America and Southeast Asia. In Cambodia, you can buy large whole roasted spiders at markets and eat them as a snack. In the Amazon rain forest, people cook huge tarantulas by squeezing their insides out onto a leaf, folding the leaf over to make a packet, and cooking it over hot embers.

A Thai zebra tarantula, which is a popular food in Cambodia.

DID YOU KNOW?

Although they're big, tarantulas move quite slowly, so they are among the easiest spiders to catch.

YUCK FACTOR!

A big hairy tarantula is revolting enough to look at, let alone to eat.

TASTY TARANTULAS

Eating a spider is a bit like eating a crab, with soft, pale meat in the head and legs. But in large spiders, the body contains a runny goop—even when cooked—containing the internal organs. Disgusting!

TOP TIP! To avoid eating the spider's fangs, they can be snipped off with scissors before cooking. Some people even use them as toothpicks!

Fried tarantulas with noodles, served in Thailand.

TRIPE

Tripe is made from an animal's stomach lining (usually a cow's). It's a kind of "offal"—meat made of organs, such as brains, lungs, and heart. Some people find tripe extra-revolting because of its vomitlike smell and spongy, rubbery texture. It's a traditional food in England and France, and in Turkey, where they make tripe soup.

YUCK FACTOR!

Compared to some of the more terrifying foods in this section, you'd probably rather eat tripe.

DON'T FORGET TO WASH IT!

Before humans can eat it, tripe has to be very well washed, since in its natural state it is coated with acidic stomach slime mixed with whatever the animal has been eating. Unwashed tripe is used as pet food for cats and dogs and is sometimes called "green tripe"—animals like cows eat mainly grass, so their stomach contents are green. Lovely!

BOILED TO BITS

Once it's washed, tripe has to be boiled for hours to make it soft enough to chew. Some people say it tastes rotten and feels like glue or snot. But others love its silky, squishy softness. It's also high in protein, low in fat, and very cheap, which explains why it's always been a popular meal.

DID YOU KNOW?

There are different types of tripe, depending on which of a cow's several stomachs it comes from. They are named after their shapes, and include honeycomb tripe and pocket tripe. Mmm!

A bowl of well-boiled tripe served and ready to eat.

TOP TIP! The traditional British way to serve tripe is boiled with milk and onions.

SHEEP'S HEAD

Imagine you sit down for dinner and there on your plate is a whole sheep's head. This lovely delicacy is eaten in the Middle East, parts of Africa, and Scandinavian countries such as Iceland and Norway, where it is a Christmas specialty.

YUCK FACTOR!

As long as you can get over it looking at you, a sheep's head could actually be quite tasty.

WHY?

You may not think of a head as providing much meat, since it's mostly bones, teeth, skin, hair, and gristle. But there is quite a lot of meat on an animal's head. You can eat the ears, the cheeks, the flesh covering the skull, the brains, the tongue, and of course the eyeballs.

HOW IS IT COOKED?

To prepare a sheep's head, you have to wash it well, scrape off the hair, salt it, and soak it in water. Then you can boil it for several hours with chopped vegetables, or roast it in an oven. It's often served with potatoes or crusty bread and a tomato or onion sauce.

BEST BITS

People who enjoy eating sheep's heads often claim that the tongue and brains are the tastiest parts, though for some the eyes are the best treats of all (see page 69).

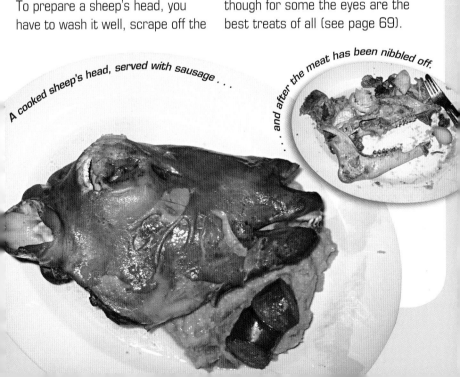

A cooked sheep's head, served with sausage . . .

. . . and after the meat has been nibbled off.

ROTTEN EGGS

Some people have a disgusting habit—forgetting to throw old food away. Beware! The smell of rotten eggs is one of the worst in the world. If you accidentally break a bad egg and get it on your hands or clothes, it's truly disgusting.

GERM INVASION

Eggs can last quite a long time without going bad—several weeks or even months. Their hard shell, lined with a stretchy, skinlike membrane, is very good at keeping germs out. But as an egg gets older, especially if it has any tiny cracks in it, bacteria can get inside it. Like any rotting food, the egg starts to change as the bacteria feed on it and give off toxic waste chemicals.

A rotten egg broken into a jar of water. The lid helps keep the smell in!

GASSY EGGS

One of the main chemicals that is released when an egg rots is called hydrogen sulfide. It is this gas that has the classic "rotten egg" smell. The same gas is also found in farts!

DID YOU KNOW?

If an egg is really rotten, it will smell and feel very light. As it dries up, a stinky gas fills the shell. Before that, you can tell how fresh an egg is by putting it in a bowl of water. If it is fresh, it will sink. If it floats, that means it is filling up with gas and has started to go bad.

TOP TIP! To keep eggs fresh, store them inside their box, in the fridge. And never eat a cracked egg!

YUCK FACTOR!

Rotten eggs are really foul—but at least no one considers them a food!

1,000-YEAR-OLD EGGS

An egg that's well past its sell-by date can be truly revolting. Yet smelly duck or chicken eggs, covered in mud and left until they turn into gray, gooey jelly, are a Chinese delicacy. Not everyone likes them, but some people think they're delicious! Because they look so ancient, they're known as 1,000-year-old eggs, or sometimes "century eggs."

WHAT REALLY HAPPENS?

A 1,000-year-old egg is not really 1,000 years old, or even 100 years old. In fact, these eggs take just a few weeks or months to make. Traditionally, they were covered in natural clay, but today century egg makers add other things such as salt and quicklime to the mix. The eggs can also be made by soaking them in a special salty liquid.

Inside, the eggs change, but do not actually rot. The covering stops bacteria from invading them, and they do not "go bad" like a normal rotten egg. The white becomes a firm jelly, and the yolk turns to a gray, creamy, cheeselike substance. A 1,000-year-old egg may taste OK, but it does smell bad. These eggs have a strong odor of ammonia from the chemicals used to make them.

Century eggs for sale at a market in China.

TOP TIP! It's best to serve 1,000-year-old eggs with pickled ginger, soy sauce, or tofu.

BEE LARVAE

Bee larvae (baby bees) are often eaten in Japan and other Asian countries. They are a good insect food if you're squeamish, because before they become adults, they don't have any wriggly legs, stingers, wings, or feelers to put you off.

A plate of bee larvae cooked and served with an herb garnish.

SWEET AS HONEY

Baby bees grow inside a bees' hive, or nest, one inside each of the small hexagonal chambers, or "cells," that the bees build. The adults feed the larvae on sweet nectar and pollen from flowers, and many people who try bee larvae say that they have a sweet, honeylike taste.

Bee larvae live in hexagon-shaped cells, and worker bees bring them food.

BEE BOUNTY

Bee larvae can be collected from the wild or grown in hives. In some places, such as rural Thailand, finding a wild bees' nest means a special treat—fresh honey and fat, tasty bee larvae, too. In Japan, baby bees are big business, and you can buy jars and cans of them in supermarkets, and order them in bars and restaurants.

YUCK FACTOR!

This is probably the least disgusting of all insect snacks.

RECIPES

Here are just a few of the ways bee larvae can be cooked:

- Fried with salt and pepper and served as a snack
- Cooked in a mixture of soy sauce and sugar
- Made into a stew with chilies
- Mixed into an omelet
- Or you can just pick them out of the hive and eat them raw!

MOOSE NOSE

Moose nose is a Canadian and Inuit specialty. It sounds as if it might be just a descriptive name for a dish, like a Yule log or mud pie (neither contain actual logs or mud). But no, it's just what it says it is—a real moose's nose, skinned, boiled, and sliced.

YUCK FACTOR!

As long as you steer clear of any snot, this is a delicious delicacy!

WHAT IS A MOOSE?

A moose is a large member of the deer family. Moose live in North America, where they are often hunted for their skin and meat. Moose have unusually long, big noses, and it's said to be the tastiest part of them.

PREPARING THE FEAST

To cook a moose nose, you have to chop the nose and upper lip off the moose head and boil them for a couple of hours until it's easy to remove the thick skin and hairs. Then you boil them again with salt, pepper, vegetables, and herbs. You can eat the sliced-up meat with sauce, or pour jelly over it and leave it to set, making "moose nose jelly." The taste is a little like strongly flavored, fatty beef.

A moose's nose where it is supposed to be—attached to its owner.

ANT STITCHES

Instead of just eating ants, why not use their biting jaws as stitches when you cut yourself? This is how some people in East Africa use a type of ant called the safari ant.

SAFARI SOLDIERS

A safari ant colony contains several different types of ant, such as soldiers who defend the colony against enemies. They have large heads and very big, powerful jaws. When they bite, they don't let go, even if they are killed.

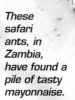

These safari ants, in Zambia, have found a pile of tasty mayonnaise.

SECURE STITCHES

Though the soldier safari ant's bite is painful, it's very useful for closing up gashes and injuries, in the same way that stitches and sutures are used in hospitals. You hold the cut closed, then hold a soldier ant up to the wound so that it bites the edges together. Then you simply snap off the rest of the ant's body, leaving the jaws in place. They can stay there for up to a week.

TOP TIP! If termites eat your crops, you can use safari ants to get rid of them. They attack the termites and drive them away.

DID YOU KNOW?

Safari ants can swarm in huge numbers, marching through villages and farmland. They don't move fast, so it's possible to run away—but they have been known to devour people who get trapped and can't move.

The powerful jaws of a safari ant.

A safari ant in action.

COBWEBS

No haunted house or spooky dungeon is complete without trails of floaty, dusty, sticky, fly-filled cobwebs dangling in your face. Even small cobwebs on ceilings are creepy, but some people don't brush them away!

SPIDER SILK

Cobwebs are made of fine threads of spider silk, which spiders make using special organs in their abdomens. The silk starts out as a jellylike liquid, but as it stretches out, it becomes a strand. Spiders use threads of silk to dangle on, and weave them together to make nests, line their tunnels, or spin webs for catching insects.

STRETCHY AND STICKY

Spider silk is incredibly strong, stretchy, and sticky. This helps webs hold together in wind and rain and cling tight to insects that get caught in them. It also explains why cobwebs can catch on your skin and stick to your face when you walk into them. And because many people are scared of spiders, they find cobwebs horrifying or revolting.

This might be one of the biggest communal spiderwebs ever found. It was created by spiders from several different species in Lake Tawakoni State Park, Texas.

YUCK FACTOR!

It's horrible if it sticks to your face, but a cobweb can't hurt you.

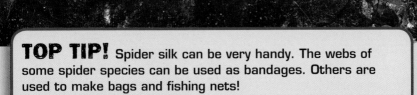

TOP TIP! Spider silk can be very handy. The webs of some spider species can be used as bandages. Others are used to make bags and fishing nets!

DUST

Everyone knows what dust looks like—but what about close up? You'll be disgusted to discover some of its most common ingredients.

BODY BITS

Household dust contains a lot of human bits, including dead skin flakes, hairs, and pieces of scabs and toenails. It also contains pet hairs and parts of creepy-crawlies, such as flies' eyes, old spider legs, and dead dust mites and their droppings (see page 57).

A scuzzy dustball of pet hairs, body bits, dead insects, and dust mite dung.

DANGEROUS DUST

Dust can be bad for you. It often contains pollen grains from plants, which can give people hay fever, and may hold tiny particles of poisonous lead from old paint and car exhaust.

DID YOU KNOW?

Your nose and throat are lined with tiny, hair-shaped parts called cilia. When you breathe in dust, they sweep it back out with rippling, waving movements.

TOP TIP! If you wipe up dust with a dry cloth or duster, you just spread it around in the air and end up breathing it in. A wet cloth is better, since it catches the dust.

BLACK MOLD

When you see something black and patchy growing in circles on a bathroom ceiling, in a shower stall, or in a damp cellar, that's black mold. It looks disgusting and dirty, but it's worse than that. It can be a killer!

DAMP AND DELICIOUS

Black mold just loves growing in damp places. That's why it appears in cellars, in bathrooms, and often on wet windowsills, where condensation runs down windowpanes and collects at the bottom. The mold has roots that reach deep into tile mortar, brick, or plaster, making it very difficult to remove.

SICKLY SPORES

Mold is a type of fungus, related to mushrooms—and, like mushrooms, it releases tiny, seedlike spores. Mold spores float in the air and can cause allergies and asthma. Mold can also release poisonous chemicals that can be deadly—though you would have to have an extremely moldy house for it to get that bad.

YUCK FACTOR!

Mold might not seem like a big problem, but it can be really revolting.

This damp, dirty bathroom corner is a perfect home for black mold.

TOP TIP! You can avoid mold if you keep surfaces dry and let fresh air into your house.

DID YOU KNOW?
Occasionally, mold spores can settle inside people's throats and lungs and collect there! Yuck!

This mold has grown and grown to form a large, yucky clump.

SPIT

Spit, or saliva, is an everyday thing. It's in our mouths all the time, and we need it to help us chew and swallow. Yet spitting is seen as one of the rudest, most disgusting things you can do. Why?

Athletes often spit on the field or sidelines to clear out their throats.

DID YOU KNOW?

In experiments, people are very reluctant to drink water that has spit in it, even if it's only their own spit!

YUCK FACTOR!

Strangely, although it's harmless, spitting is extremely disgusting and upsetting for many people.

WHAT IS SPIT?

Your mouth releases saliva all the time, from small organs called salivary glands around your tongue. Saliva is mostly made of water, along with some chemicals that help dissolve food. Our mouths need to be wet in order to taste, to chew and swallow food, and to talk easily.

I SPIT AT YOU!

So why do we find spitting so disgusting? In most cultures, spitting at someone is a way of insulting them. It could be something to do with disease germs being carried in our saliva. If you spit at someone, you are giving them any germs you might have.

UGH! I CAN'T SWALLOW THIS!

We also find it disgusting to see people spit out food or spit into a drink. It's our instinct to spit things out if they are poisonous or rotten, so that could explain why seeing someone spit makes you feel queasy.

In parts of Asia, many people like to chew a mixture of betel leaves and areca nuts, then spit them out. The spit is bright red, leaving colorful splats on the ground.

SWEATY FEET

Pheeww-y! The smell of sweaty feet can have you holding your nose from the other side of the room. It's even worse if sweaty, stinky socks are left in a heap for days or weeks on end. The longer they wait for a wash, the smellier they get.

SO WHAT IS SWEAT?

Sweat is a liquid, mainly made of water, released from our skin. As it evaporates into the air, it cools us down. Sweat also keeps our skin from drying out, and being slightly damp helps our hands to grip things. Sweat itself doesn't actually smell much. But bacteria on our skin feed on it and give out smelly substances. So after a while, we start to stink.

WHY ARE FEET SWEATY?

Sweat comes from tiny glands in the skin. Feet have loads of sweat glands—around 250,000 each! Our feet move and bend all day long, and keeping them damp stops the skin from cracking. Feet also sweat to help them grip. Before socks and shoes, people walked, ran, and climbed trees and rocks in bare feet, so sweaty feet were useful.

Don't get too close! Unwashed feet like these are usually the stinkiest of all.

YUCK FACTOR!

Sweaty feet can smell, but they're usually fixed with a quick wash.

DID YOU KNOW?

In one single day, an adult man's feet can produce more than two cupfuls (500 mL) of sweat!

BURPS

BUUURRRPP! Excuse me! In many cultures, burping (or belching) is considered rude, especially if you do a loud, smelly belch at the dinner table. In some countries, however, such as China and Ghana, a belch can be acceptable, because it means you enjoyed your food.

WHAT IS A BURP?

We burp to let trapped gases escape from our stomachs. Sometimes, air gets into the stomach when we eat, and that can cause a belch. You'll burp even more if you have a fizzy drink, as it contains lots of carbon dioxide gas. As the gas escapes, it makes the top of your esophagus vibrate, making the familiar burping sound.

Drinking down a fizzy drink quickly is a great way to achieve long and noisy burps!

STINKY BURPS

It doesn't smell great inside most people's stomachs, thanks to the mixture of mashed-up food and strong stomach acid. Burps often carry this smell out with them, making them extra-disgusting.

YUCK FACTOR!

You'll have to say "excuse me," but burping isn't really that bad.

DID YOU KNOW?

Paul Hunn from the UK claimed the world record for the loudest burp ever in 2008, with a burp of just over 107 decibels. That's as loud as a subway train!

TOP TIP! If you want to avoid burping, eat your food slowly and don't gulp it.

FLATULENCE

There are certainly many things ruder than burping, and one of them is breaking wind. It happens when smelly gas escapes from you—usually making a loud and embarrassing noise.

Who did that? Intestinal gas can smell reeaally bad.

GAS IN YOUR GUTS

Like burping, breaking wind is just a way of letting gas out of your body. Before it comes out, the gas collects in your guts, or intestines—the long tubes that lead out of your stomach.

WHY DOES WIND SMELL?

Gas from fizzy drinks can make you flatulent. But more often, gas gathers in your intestines when bacteria and yeast inside you digest foods such as beans. As they break down the food, they give out gases, which often have a strong smell.

DID YOU KNOW?

Though many people find breaking wind terribly rude, it's completely normal and everyone does it. Most people release roughly a pint (half a liter) of gas in total every day.

YUCK FACTOR!

We all do it, but it's still really revolting.

TOP TIP! Gas-causing foods include beans, lentils, onions, and cabbage.

SNOT

Snot, bogeys, boogers, or greenies—everyone with a nose knows about the crispy, dried bits of mucus that collect up there. It's tempting to pick them, but let anyone see you and you'll be met with shouts of "Ewww!"

WHAT'S SNOT FOR?

Snot starts out as liquid mucus, a runny, sticky substance produced by many parts of your body. Nasal (or nose) mucus keeps the inside of your nose damp, and traps germs and pollution to stop them from getting inside you. It even contains germ-killing chemicals. Boogers are dried, hardened bits of nasal mucus, mixed with bacteria, dust, pollen, and pollution.

PICK IT? EAT IT?

Eating snot isn't THAT gross—we actually swallow small amounts of it all the time as it trickles down the backs of our throats. But picking dried snot out is seen as more disgusting—especially if you eat it, too. However, surveys suggest that almost everyone picks their nose sometimes, even if only in secret.

Of course, the polite thing to do is to collect your snot discreetly in a tissue.

YUCK FACTOR!

It can't be THAT revolting if most of us manage to pick our noses!

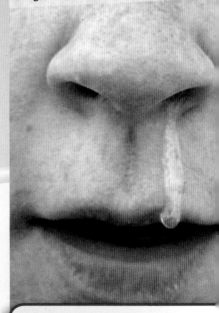

Before snot dries to make crispy boogers, it's runny, slimy, and gloppy.

DID YOU KNOW?

Scientists have found that eating snot isn't harmful, and could even be good for you. When they reach your stomach, germs in the snot may help to strengthen your body's immune (germ-fighting) system.

TOP TIP!
Picking your nose too much can be bad for you, as it makes the inside of your nose sore. So take care!

PHLEGM

You don't normally see phlegm, but you may know what it looks like if you've been ill. It's the gooey, greenish or yellowish stuff that comes out of your throat when you have a bad cough or chest infection.

ALWAYS THERE

You actually have a thin layer of clear phlegm, or mucus, lining your throat and breathing tubes at all times. It catches bits of dust and germs to keep them out of your lungs. When you have a chest or throat illness, your body makes extra, thicker phlegm containing white blood cells, which fight germs. Tiny molecules in these cells make the phlegm look yellow or green!

WHY IS IT DISGUSTING?

The sight of a yucky, quivering, jellylike blob of green phlegm can make most people feel revolted, partly because of its slimy, wobbly texture. We are probably also instinctively afraid of phlegm because it appears when people are ill, so touching it could mean catching germs.

TOP TIP! Milk and dairy products can make phlegm thicker and yuckier, so don't have too much of them when you have a cold.

YUCK FACTOR!

Ugh! There's something about a blob of green phlegm that's truly stomach-turning.

SIGNS IN THE PHLEGM

Phlegm is actually very useful for doctors. It can contain clues about lung illnesses. For example, blood in the phlegm can be a sign of a serious disease called tuberculosis.

When you have a nasty cold or flu, you could cough up a jellylike lump of phlegm like this.

EARWAX

YUCK FACTOR!

Compared to some revolting body bits, earwax is no big deal.

All the time, the insides of your ears are churning out earwax. It smells funny, and tastes even worse, but it's actually very important.

WAXY AND CLEAN

Earwax comes from tiny glands in your ear canal (the tube leading into your ear). It prevents the skin inside the ears from drying out and traps dust and germs. It also contains acidic chemicals that kill germs. (If this didn't happen, everyone would get painful, damaging ear infections all the time.) As you move your jaw when you speak and eat, the earwax gradually works its way out of your ears.

WHAT'S IT LIKE?

There are two types of earwax. People with an Asian or Native American background usually have drier, flakier earwax that is grayish in color, while people with a European or African background have stickier, wetter, brown or yellow earwax. Earwax smells waxy and cheesy, and if you're unlucky enough to get it in your mouth, it tastes very bitter.

DID YOU KNOW?

Scientists can tell how old a whale is by counting the layers of earwax inside its ears. (Bet you didn't even know whales had ears!)

This earwax is the sticky, gluey, yellow type.

TOP TIP! Never stick anything in your ears to try to pick out earwax. If too much wax collects, a doctor can rinse it out using a water-filled syringe.

EYE GUNK

When you wake up in the morning, there's often a bit of strange crusty stuff in the corners of your eyes. Some people call it eye gunk, sleepydust, just "sleep," or eye boogers! Scientists call it "rheum." But what is it?

SLEEPYDUST

Your eyes constantly leak out a little bit of rheum. It's a liquid mixture of tears, mucus, dust that gets into your eyes, and dead body cells. During the day, it gets washed away as your eyes open and close. But at night, your eyes stay shut for many hours, so the rheum collects in the corners. It dries out and forms crusty, sandy, brownish clumps.

THE SANDMAN

In fairy tales and folklore, the Sandman is a magical visitor who sprinkles sleeping sand onto children's eyes to help them sleep and give them pleasant dreams. This idea comes from the rheum or "eye sand" that appears in the eyes every morning.

The Sandman sprinkles sleepy sand in this illustration.

YUCK FACTOR!

This crunchy, crusty gunk isn't all that revolting.

TOO CRUSTY!

A little bit of rheum is normal and healthy. But if you have so much that it's sealing your eyes shut in the morning, or if your eyes are itchy and sore, it can be a sign of an eye infection or disease.

Most of us have a bit of eye gunk each morning.

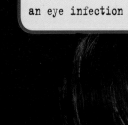

THE SANDMAN

SCABS

When you get a cut or a scrape, your body immediately starts fixing it. It makes your blood clot, or harden, and seals over the wound with a protective scab. Scabs aren't gross, really—they're good news. But picking scabs is definitely disgusting.

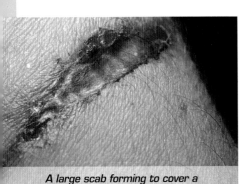

A large scab forming to cover a wound on someone's leg.

DID YOU KNOW?

In 2003, a man who was lost in a jungle in Colombia for 12 days without food was forced to eat a large scab that formed after he cut his chin on a rock. Yum! Eating scabs won't hurt you, and it was a good idea in this case. But it's still pretty disgusting.

YUCK FACTOR!

Scabs are superhelpful, but picking them and eating them is gross.

NATURAL BAND-AID

A scab is a natural cover for a wound. It's made from bits of blood cells bound together with a stringy body chemical called fibrin. The scab keeps germs out and protects the cut until it's healed over. Then, the scab finally falls off by itself—as long as you don't pick it!

DON'T TOUCH THAT SCAB!

Most people have given in to the temptation to pick a scab. A scab often feels itchy, which means the wound is healing—but it can make you want to pick it. You might want to pick a scab just to see what's underneath. But don't do it! Picking scabs can make your wound open and bleed. Then you'll get a bigger scab and could be left with a scar. Even worse, germs could get in and infect the cut, making you ill.

TOP TIP! You can sometimes stop a scab from itching by rubbing Vaseline on it.

PUS

If your body's making pus, it's a sure sign that germs have gotten in. This gloppy yellow substance is made when germs invade the body and germ-killing cells go into battle with them.

INFECTED WOUNDS

The main place you'll see pus is in a cut or other wound, after germs have gotten in. It looks like creamy yellow mayonnaise around or inside the wound, and it can smell revoltingly cheesy. Yuck! An infected wound may also look swollen and red, and feel painful.

BOILS, ZITS, AND ABSCESSES

Sometimes, bacteria finds its way under the skin. This could happen around the root of a hair, for example. Germ-killing cells gather and pus forms, but it can't escape—so it builds up under pressure to form a painful lump. If this is just under the skin, it forms a pimple that eventually pops, and the pus comes out. But if it's deep under the skin, it forms a big boil or abscess. These can make people seriously ill, and they sometimes have to go to the hospital to have them removed. Ouch!

YUCK FACTOR!

Pus can be revolting, because it's associated with illness and germs.

TOP TIP! It's a bad idea to squeeze the pus out of pimples, or zits. You could force it deeper under your skin, or damage the skin and leave a scar.

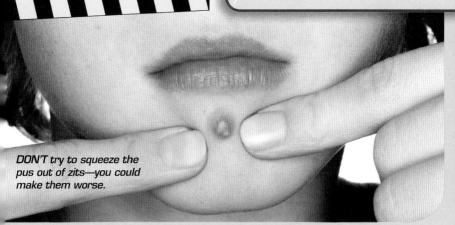

DON'T try to squeeze the pus out of zits—you could make them worse.

SNEEZING

Ah . . . ahh . . . ahhh . . . CHOO!!! **You sneeze when you have a cold or flu—but also if you get dust or pepper up your nose. Sneezing is a reflex that helps us clear out our noses—whether they're filled with too much snot or have sniffed in something irritating.**

HOW A SNEEZE WORKS

A sneeze starts when something irritates the nerves inside the nose. These nerves send messages to your brain, which then sets the sneeze off. First you take a big breath, then powerful muscles in your chest force air out of your nose and mouth at a great speed.

A spray of droplets from a sneeze is caught on camera.

YUCK FACTOR!

Sneezing is only really revolting if someone sneezes right on you, instead of into a tissue!

SNEEZES SPREAD DISEASES

Sneezing sprays droplets of your snot and saliva into the air. If you're ill, this can spread your cough, cold, or flu germs far and wide. In fact, some germs make you sneeze as a way of ensuring they spread easily from one person to another.

TOP TIP! You can sometimes prevent a sneeze by stretching your upper lip downward over your front teeth or pressing your upper lip firmly.

DID YOU KNOW?

Bright lights make some people sneeze. No one knows the reason for this.

VOMIT

Vomiting is horrible! Whether it's caused by a stomach bug or a dizzying roller coaster, hurling up a mixture of mashed-up food and stinky stomach acid through your mouth and nose is vile. It makes you cough and choke, and it tastes and smells hideous. So why do we do it?

GET THIS OUT OF HERE!

Your body uses vomiting to get dangerous stuff out of your stomach. Germs, poison, or food that's gone bad can all make you throw up. It's unpleasant, but your body does it to save you from something even worse—illness or even death caused by something you've eaten.

ALL SICK TOGETHER

Seeing or even just hearing someone throw up can make other people around them sick, too. This is actually useful—it means that if everyone's eaten the same bad food, everyone can get rid of it.

FEELING DIZZY

Why do people get motion sickness from going on a ride at an amusement park, being on a boat, or even just riding in a car? Scientists think that if you sway or whirl around, your brain gets mixed messages from your eyes and from the balancing system in your ears, making you feel dizzy. This is like what some poisons do to you—they make you feel dizzy and confused. So your body may decide you're being poisoned and make you vomit.

Vomiting serves a useful purpose but feels terrible.

TOP TIP! To avoid motion sickness, try to lock your eyes onto a fixed point, such as the horizon. This makes your brain less confused.

PEE

If this person's pee doesn't get washed away soon, it will really start to smell.

Everybody has to go to the bathroom several times a day to let out pee, or urine. It's not too smelly to start with. But if you've ever smelled week-old pee splashed around a toilet, you'll know that it has a disgusting smell!

LIQUID IN, LIQUID OUT

We have to drink liquid regularly to keep our bodies filled with water. (A human body is around 60 percent water!) Urine is a mixture of spare water and waste chemicals that need to be flushed out from the body.

HOW DOES IT WORK?

Your blood is constantly being filtered through two organs called kidneys. It only takes 45 minutes for them to filter all the blood in your body! As they do so, they collect spare water and waste chemicals, including a toxic chemical called urea. Urea is smelly, especially when it starts to break down into other chemicals, or when germs collect in it. That's why the longer urine hangs around, the stinkier it gets.

DID YOU KNOW?

When pee first comes out, it's superclean. Unlike poo, it contains no germs at all. People lost in the desert have survived by drinking their urine—though this isn't a great idea, since urea is not very good for you.

TOP TIP! Drinking plenty of water keeps your kidneys working well.

POO

Dog poo on the street. Watch where you put your feet!

Everyone has to poo, and yet we find poo deeply disgusting. We're right to find it gross, though, because poo can contain dangerous disease germs. Recoiling from it and washing it away keeps us safe and healthy.

WHAT IS POO?

Poo (scientifically known as feces) is partly made of leftover food, especially the bits that our bodies can't digest well, such as fruit and vegetable skins and seed husks. They are mixed with a bit of water and millions of bacteria that live naturally in our intestines. It's these bacteria that give poo its horribly stinky smell. As the poo travels along inside your intestines, it is also coated with slippery mucus to help it leave your body in a nice, neat fashion.

This photo from Bangladesh shows cow dung (poo) being dried in the sun to make fuel.

YUCK FACTOR!

Though it's natural, most people find poo the most revolting thing of all.

TOP TIP! Always wash your hands after using the toilet! You knew that—but why? Germs in poo, which are harmless in your intestines, can poison you if they get on your food and into your stomach. You can also catch other people's diseases from germs in their poo.

DID YOU KNOW?

Although poo is a waste substance, it still contains some useful food. Some flies, beetles, and other bugs like to eat poo.

TOILET

In modern cities, most homes have a nice, shiny flush toilet. It collects pee, poo, and other disgusting stuff such as vomit, and you can flush it all away into the sewer.

FLUSH TOILETS
Proper flushing toilets were first invented in 1594, but it was almost 300 years later before they became widespread. A flush toilet has a water tank connected to the bowl that you sit on. When you flush, the tank releases the water into the bowl, which washes everything away down another pipe known as a siphon.

LIFE WITHOUT TOILETS
Toilets may seem a bit gross, but they're lovely compared to the alternative! Before flush toilets and sewers, people had to do their poos and pees somewhere else. They could dig a pit some distance from their homes and go there. (This still happens in some parts of the world.) During medieval times and even up until the 1600s, people living in cities used a bowl called a chamber pot (usually made of china) and simply emptied it into the street. Compared to this, a proper toilet seems positively delightful.

YUCK FACTOR!
Toilets can be gross, but life would be much smellier without them.

In many parts of the world where water is very scarce, some toilets don't use flushing water, just the force of gravity.

A sewage plant, where waste from modern flush toilets is processed.

ANCIENT TOILETS
The ancient Romans, and the people of the ancient Indus Valley civilization in India, had early toilets thousands of years ago. The toilets didn't have modern water tanks, but instead emptied into a sewerlike channel and were flushed with a flow of clean water.

SEWER

YUCK FACTOR!

If you stepped inside a sewer right now, it would be seriously revolting.

When you flush your toilet, spit out your toothpaste, or throw sour milk down your kitchen sink, where does it all go? Into the sewers—a network of tunnels under the streets. They carry human waste away to be cleaned up and treated. And as you can imagine, they're not a nice place to be.

SEWER SOUP

If you think about everything that you flush or rinse away, you'll realize that a sewer contains a lot of revolting stuff. Floating along in a stream of dirty water and pee are poo, vomit, bits of rotten food, mud, chunks of rancid, hardened frying fat from restaurants, strong cleaning chemicals, and even dirty diapers (you are not supposed to put these down the toilet, but some people do). As these things mix together and rot, they give off stinky gases, too.

TAKE IT AWAY!

They may be gross, but of course having sewers is actually good news. They remove waste from where we live, helping us stay clean and healthy. When sewage reaches a treatment plant, the waste is treated and filtered to make it safe. The waste is often then released into the sea. Some elements may be refined and recycled for use in farming or for other industrial use.

BEASTS OF THE SEWERS

You may have heard tales of escaped turtles or crocodiles roaming around in city sewers. Actually, this hardly ever happens—but sewers are home to thousands of hungry rats, which feed on the bits of smelly food.

In this open sewer in India, waste flows between the houses.

TOOTH PLAQUE

A close-up of tooth plaque bacteria seen under a microscope.

TOP TIP! Obviously, if you want to reduce plaque, you have to brush your teeth often and floss them, too. Avoiding sticky, sugary foods and chewing sugarless gum can also help.

In 1683, Dutchman Antonie van Leeuwenhoek, who had invented an early microscope, described how he had used it to look at his own tooth plaque. To his amazement he saw "many very little living animalcules, very prettily a-moving." Something was living on his teeth!

WHAT IS PLAQUE?

Tooth plaque is a slimy substance that builds up in a layer all over your teeth if you don't brush them enough. It is actually made of millions of tiny bacteria feeding on old food, especially sugar, left on your teeth. These are the little wriggling "animalcules" (or tiny animals) that Van Leeuwenhoek saw.

EATING YOUR TEETH

A few of these germs actually live naturally in your mouth and are normally harmless. But if you let a thick layer of plaque build up, the bacteria give off a kind of acid as they feed on sugar. This acid can start to eat away at your teeth, causing tooth decay.

Healthy tooth

Plaque bacteria can damage the gums and bones around your teeth.

Healthy gums

Healthy bone

Plaque

Tartar

Reduced bone level

Gum and bone damage

TOOTH DECAY

If you don't clean your teeth properly to get rid of tooth plaque, tooth decay can set in. "Decay" means rotting, and it's true—your teeth can literally rot away into blackened, smelly, and very painful stumps. Yuck! Luckily, a dentist should be able to step in before that happens.

HOW IT WORKS

Your teeth are covered with an incredibly hard substance called enamel. It protects them from damage and lets you crunch hard nuts and candy. But one thing it can't cope with is acid made by the bacteria in tooth plaque, which slowly dissolves the tooth enamel away.

YUCK FACTOR!

If left untreated, rotten teeth can get really nasty.

TOOTH INVASION!

Once there's a hole in the enamel, germs can get into the softer part inside your tooth, making it start to rot. It turns a dark blackish brown color and also smells nasty. A dentist can drill away the decay and replace the missing bit with a filling. Otherwise, the rot will reach the nerve inside your tooth and it will REALLY hurt. Ouch!

Several of this person's teeth are decaying badly.

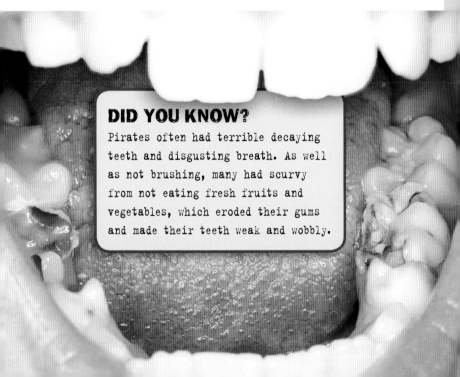

DID YOU KNOW?

Pirates often had terrible decaying teeth and disgusting breath. As well as not brushing, many had scurvy from not eating fresh fruits and vegetables, which eroded their gums and made their teeth weak and wobbly.

SPIDER BITE

First of all, don't panic! Most spiders don't bite people. And even if they do, most spider bites are not dangerous. However, a few spider species have a truly dangerous bite that can make your skin and flesh start to wither and rot away. Yikes!

WHICH SPIDERS? WHERE ARE THEY?!

Only two main types of spiders can cause this rotting, or "necrosis," with their bites. They are the recluse spiders, found mainly in the Americas, and six-eyed sand spiders from southern Africa. None of these spiders are likely to bite you. They usually only bite if they get squashed or trapped in clothes or bed linen.

WHAT HAPPENS?

A bite from one of these dangerous spiders, such as the brown recluse, is often minor. You may not even feel it. But sometimes, the skin becomes itchy and painful. In some people, a large wound gradually forms and necrosis begins. This damaged area of flesh is known as a "volcano lesion" and can be as large as a human hand! The wound does eventually heal over, but full recovery could take months.

A bite from a brown recluse spider can develop into a horrible wound.

TOP TIP! If one of these spiders bites you, keep the bite site clean and covered, use an ice pack to cool it down, and call a doctor if it starts to hurt or itch.

ARE THEY KILLERS?

Some of these spiders can be deadly, but only very rarely.

SNAKEBITE

There are many different kinds of venomous snakes, and many different kinds of horrible snakebites that can cause terrible swelling, necrosis (flesh rotting), blistering, and scarring. Some of the pictures are so scary we can't even put them in this book!

The black mamba, an extremely dangerous snake from Africa.

ROTTING AWAY

Like the bite of the recluse spider, some snakebites make your flesh rot away. This happens most often with snakes in the viper family, such as rattlesnakes and bushmasters. They can cause a large wound to open up or even make an entire hand, foot, or arm rot away.

SWELLING AND BLISTERING

If you're lucky, a snakebite won't cause necrosis, just swelling. A hand could swell to twice its size and be covered with huge, bubblelike blisters.

TOP TIP! If you ever see a snake, stay calm and back away quietly. Do NOT try to poke it, scare it, or pick it up! Many snakes have dangerous bites, and it's not always easy to tell what type of snake you have found.

YUCK FACTOR!

A snakebite could make part of your body completely unrecognizable.

Following a snake bite, this person's leg swelled up and had to be operated on.

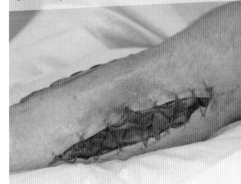

LOSING A LIMB

Sometimes, in places that are far from a hospital, the best way to save a snakebite victim is to remove the arm or leg that has been bitten.

MAGGOT THERAPY

You've got a nasty, gangrenous wound that's smelling bad and failing to heal. What do the doctors do? Wrap it up in a bandage filled with live, wriggling, hungry maggots? Of course not! Well, actually, they do. . . .

HUNGRY FOR DEAD FLESH

Maggots are baby flies (see pages 11–12). Some species feed only on the flesh of dead animals, growing bigger and fatter until they are ready to turn into adult flies. That's actually good news if you have gangrene, which means that some of your flesh is dying and rotting. Maggots nibble away the dead bits, stopping the rot from spreading, and leaving the wound clean and ready to heal.

These hungry maggots are nibbling their way through a meaty lunch.

YUCK FACTOR!

Putting maggots in a wound seems utterly gross, even if it is good for you.

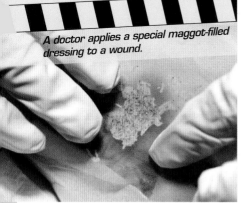
A doctor applies a special maggot-filled dressing to a wound.

APPLYING MAGGOTS

Medical maggots are not collected from dead animals found lying around—they're specially bred and free of germs. To make sure they can breathe and move around, doctors apply them to the wound inside a loose dressing with airholes in it. They can stay in there for days!

DOES IT HURT?

Because maggots only eat dead tissue, their nibbling is a bit like having your hair or fingernails cut, and shouldn't hurt. However, some patients say that they can feel the maggots wriggling and tickling!

DID YOU KNOW?

Maggots have been used to clean wounds since ancient times. They were reintroduced into modern medicine in the 1930s.

LEECH HEALING

If your doctor doesn't decide to set maggots on you, you could get sucked by a bloodthirsty leech instead! Leeches, like maggots, are increasingly being used in medicine.

YUCK FACTOR!

Having a leech sucking you is pretty revolting, but at least it will only cling on for a few minutes.

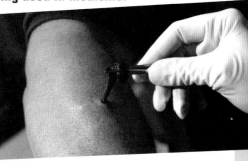

A doctor carefully applies a leech to skin after surgery.

SLURPING UP THE BLOOD

Not all leeches suck blood, but a few do. Doctors usually use a bloodsucking species called the European medicinal leech, which can grow to 8 inches (20 cm) long—as big as a banana!

This small species of leech is trying to nibble someone's toe.

WHAT'S IT USED FOR?

Because leeches suck blood, they can be used to vacuum up clogged or infected blood from wounds, leaving them cleaned and healthy. Another useful job they can do is suck blood into body parts that have been reattached—for example, fingers that have been chopped off and sewn back on. The leech is placed on the reattached part, and as it sucks it increases blood flow where the parts have been surgically joined.

LEECH GATHERERS

People used to make a living collecting leeches from ponds and swamps for doctors to use. Today, medicinal leeches are bred in special labs.

ACKNOWLEDGMENTS

The publisher thanks the following agencies and illustrators for their kind permission to use their images.

Photos
Pages: 1 Shutterstock/Werg; **2bl** Shutterstock/Vitalii Nesterchuk; **2br** Shutterstock/Paul Prescott; **2–3t** Shutterstock/Dusty Cline; **2–3 background** Shutterstock/Stacy Barnett; **3tr** Shutterstock/Sean Best; **3bl** Shutterstock/Holger W; **3br** Shutterstock/Tan Kian Khoon; **4–5** Shutterstock/Vinicius Tupinamba; **6–7** Nature/Andrew Parkinson; **7t** Becca Lewis; **8–9** Getty Images/Paul Zahl; **10** NaturePL/Kim Taylor; **11** Rex Features/Robert Harding Associates/N. A. Callow; **12** FLPA/Nigel Cattlin; **13** NHPA/Mark Bowler; **14c** NaturePL/Arco/Wegner; **15t** FLPA/Mark Moffett/Minden Pictures; **15b** Photolibrary/Robert Oelman; **16** NaturePL/Rod Clarke/John Downer Productions; **17** NaturePL/Premaphotos; **18** Science Photo Library/Gustoimages; **19t** Corbis/Robert Pickett; **19b** FLPA/Larry West; **20** Corbis/Reuters; **21** Science Photo Library/Karl H. Switak; **22** Photoshot/Oceans-Image/Norbert Wu; **23bl** Corbis/Martin Harvey; **23br** Corbis/William Radcliffe; **24** Getty Images/Yomiuri Shimbun; **25** FLPA/Minden Pictures/Flip Nicklin; **26t** FLPA/Minden Pictures/Cyril Ruoso; **26b** Ardea/Adrian Warren; **27** Photolibrary/OSF; **28** Photolibrary/Kathie Atkinson; **29** Photoshot/NHPA/Daniel Heuclin; **30t** NaturePL/Brandon Cole; **30b** Science Photo Library/Tom McHugh; **31** NOAA/NMF/NWFSC Library, Alaska Fisheries Science Center, Seattle; **32** NaturePL/Anup Shah; **33** NaturePL/Jouan Rius; **34** Photoshot/NHPA/Roger Tidman; **35t** Ardea/Adrian Warren; **35b** Corbis/Patricia Fogden; **36** Corbis/Tim Davis; **37** NaturePL/Andrew Parkinson; **38** Corbis/Joe McDonald; **39** NaturePL/Suzi Eszterhas; **40** Photolibrary/David Kirkland; **41** Getty Images/AFP/Henning Kaiser; **42** Getty Images/Paul Zahl; **43** Photoshot/NHPA/Nick Garbutt; **44** NaturePL/Jose B. Ruiz; **45t** DK Images/Neil Fletcher & Matthew Ward; **45b** Corbis/Douglas Peebles; **46** Science Photo Library/Dr. Jeremy Burgess; **47t** Kobal Collection/TRI-STAR; **47b** Photolibrary/Animals Animals/Er Degginger; **48** Corbis/Buddy Mays; **49** Ardea/Johan De Meester; **50r** Shutterstock/Jeffrey Van Daele; **51** Science Photo Library/Andrew Syred; **52** Shutterstock/David Dohnal; **53b** Corbis/Clouds Hill Imaging Ltd; **54l** Timothy Branning; **54t** NaturePL/Mark Taylor; **55** Shutterstock/pzAxe; **56** Corbis/Anthony Bannister; **57** Shutterstock/Sebastian Kaulitzki; **58** Photolibrary/James Robinson; **59** Science Photo Library/Eye of Science; **60** Corbis/Louise Gubb; **61** Dr. Nico J. Smit/Dept of Zoology, University of Johannesburg, South Africa; **62–63** Rex Features/Profile Press; **64tr** Photolibrary/Andy Stewart; **65** Carol Spears; **66t** Shutterstock/Ostill;

66b Shutterstock/Steffen Foerster Photography; **67** Getty Images/National Geographic/Randy Olson; **68t** NaturePL/Dr. Axel Gebauer; **68b** Getty Images/China Photos; **69** Shutterstock/Algecireño; **70t** Shutterstock/Ly Dinh Quoc Vu; **70bl** Marshall Editions; **70br** Shutterstock/Ly Dinh Quoc Vu; **71t** FLPA/Terry Whittaker; **71b** Getty Images/AFP/Jean-Baptiste Fauvel; **72** StockFood/Food Collection; **73t** StockFood/Fei, Wang Xiao; **73bl** Corbis/Michael Freeman; **74** Marshall Editions; **75t** Rex Features/Finlayson/Newspix; **75c** Donald Hobern/Flickr.com; **75b** Digital Vision; **76t** Science Photo Library/Peter Menzel; **76b** Science Photo Library/Jacques Jangoux; **77t** Shutterstock/Bent G. Nordeng; **77c** Photo Library/Tips Italia; **77b** Shutterstock/Bent G. Nordeng; **78b** Science Photo Library/Peter Menzel; **79t** Shutterstock/Andrey Sukhachev; **79b** Corbis/Owen Franken; **80t** Photo Library/Guy Moberly; **80b** Kent Wang, Texas; **81t&b** Gard Karlsen; **82** Alamy/Oote Boe Photography; **83** Corbis/Christine Osborne; **84t** Marshall Editions; **84b** FLPA/Gary K. Smith; **85** Shutterstock/Almondd; **86c** NaturePL/Martin Dohrn; **86b** Laura Darby; **87t** Corbis/Cusp/C. Lyttle; **87b** Brad Wofford; **88** Shutterstock/Photoroller; **89t** Alamy/Jochen Tack; **89b** Alamy/M. Hauser; **90t** Getty Images/Paul Spinelli; **90b** Shutterstock/Paul Prescott; **91bl** Shutterstock/Morgan Lane Photography; **91br** Shutterstock/Beth Van Trees; **92** Mark Dodds/Flickr.com; **93t** Shutterstock; **93c** Shutterstock/Katia Vasileva; **93bl** Shutterstock/Arina; **93br** Shutterstock/MarFot; **94t** Becca Lewis; **94b** Shutterstock/Madeleine Openshaw; **95** Erica Potechin; **96** Gregory F. Maxwell; **97bl** Mary Evans Picture Library; **97br** Shutterstock/Julie DeGuia; **98** Shutterstock/Mountain Hardcore; **99** Shutterstock/Suzanne Tucker; **100** Corbis/Science Faction/William Radcliffe; **101** Photolibrary/Roland Marske/Voller Ernst; **102** Getty Images/Kaveh Kazemi; **103t** FLPA/David Hosking; **103b** Corbis/Gideon Mendel; **104** Shutterstock/Konstantin Tavrov; **105** Corbis/Howard Davies; **106** Corbis/Science Faction/David Scharf; **107** Shutterstock/Hirlesteanu Constantin-Ciprian; **109b** Photo Library/Scott Camazine; **110t** Ardea/Jean Michel Labat; **110b** Science Photo Library/Louise Murrary; **111t** Corbis/Tony Savino.

Illustrations
Pages: 14t Marshall Editions; **53t** Marshall Editions; **84t** Shutterstock; **92 background** Shuttterstock/Lemony; **92b** Shutterstock/Blight; **94–95 background** Shutterstock; **106b** Shutterstock.